# The M
## of the
# Horseshoe

ROBERT MEANS LAWRENCE

Published by Hesperus Press Limited
28 Mortimer Street, London W1W 7RD
www.hesperuspress.com

*The Magic of the Horseshoe* first published in 1898.
First published by Hesperus Press Limited, 2015

Designed and typeset by Madeline Meckiffe
Printed and bound by CPI Group (UK) Ltd, Croydon, CR0 4YY

ISBN: 978-1-84391-562-1

# The Magic
## of the
# Horseshoe

## A Collection of Folklore,
## Myths and Superstitions

HESPERUS

*And still o'er many a neighboring door*
*She saw the horseshoe's curved charm.*

– Whittier, *The Witch's Daughter*


*Happy art thou, as if every day thou hadst picked up a horseshoe.*

– Longfellow, *Evangeline*

# CONTENTS

# THE MAGIC OF
# THE HORSESHOE

## THE HORSESHOE
## AS A SAFEGUARD

*Your wife's a witch, man; you should nail*
*a horseshoe on your chamber door.*
– Sir Walter Scott, *Redgauntlet*

As a practical device for the protection of horses' feet, the utility of the iron horseshoe has long been generally recognized; and for centuries, in countries widely separated, it has also been popularly used as a talisman for the preservation of buildings or premises from the wiles of witches and fiends.

To the student of folklore, a superstition like this, which has exerted so wide an influence over men's minds in the past, and which is also universally prevalent in our own times, must have a peculiar interest. What, then, were the reasons for the general adoption of the horseshoe as a talisman?

Among the Romans there prevailed a custom of driving nails into cottage walls as an antidote against the plague. Both this practice and the later one of nailing up horseshoes have been thought by some to originate from the rite of the Passover. The blood sprinkled upon the doorposts and lintel at the time of the great Jewish feast formed the chief points of an arch, and it may be that with this in mind people adopted the horseshoe as an arch-shaped talisman, and it thus became generally emblematic of good luck.

⋯⋯

The same thought may underlie the practice of the peasants in the west of Scotland, who train the boughs of the rowan or mountain-ash tree in the form of an arch over a farmyard gate to protect their cattle from evil.

⋯⋯

## HORNS AND OTHER TWO-PRONGED OBJECTS

The supernatural qualities of the horseshoe as a preservative against imaginary demons have been supposed to be due to its bifurcated shape, as any object having two prongs or forks was formerly thought to be effective for this purpose. As with the crescent, the source of this belief is doubtless the appearance of the moon in certain of its phases.

Hence, according to some authorities, is derived the alleged efficacy as amulets of horseshoes, the horns and tusks of animals, the talons of birds, and the claws of wild beasts, lobsters, and crabs. Hence, too, the significance of the oft-quoted lines from Robert Herrick's *Hesperides*:

> *Hang up hooks and sheers to scare*
> *Hence, the hag that rides the mare.*

———— ✷ • ✷ ————

The horn of the fabulous unicorn, in reality none other than that of the rhinoceros, is much valued as an amulet, and in west Africa, where the horns of wild animals are greatly esteemed as fiend-scarers, a large horn filled with mud and having three small horns attached to its lower end is used as a safeguard to prevent slaves from running away.

———— ✷ • ✷ ————

In the vicinity of Mirzapur in central Hindustan the Horwas tie on the necks of their children the roots of jungle plants as protective charms; their efficacy being thought to depend on their resemblance to the horns of certain wild beasts.

The Mohammedans of northern India use a complex amulet, composed in part of a tiger's claw and two claws of the large-horned owl with the tips facing outward, while in southern Europe we find the necks of mules ornamented with two boar's tusks or with the horns of an antelope.

———— ✷ • ✷ ————

Amulets fashioned in the shape of horns and crescents are very popular among the Neapolitans. Mr Frederick Thomas Elworthy quotes at some length from the *Mimica degli antichi* of Andrea de Jorio in illustration of this fact. From this source we learn that the horns of Sicilian oxen and of bullocks are in favor with the nobility and aristocracy as evil-eye protectives, and are frequently seen on their houses and in their gardens; stag's antlers are the favorites with grocers and chemists, while the lower classes are content with the horns of rams and goats. The Sicilians are wont to tie pieces of red ribbon to the little horns which they wear as charms, and this is supposed vastly to increase their efficiency.

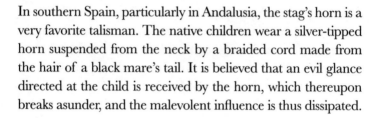

In southern Spain, particularly in Andalusia, the stag's horn is a very favorite talisman. The native children wear a silver-tipped horn suspended from the neck by a braided cord made from the hair of a black mare's tail. It is believed that an evil glance directed at the child is received by the horn, which thereupon breaks asunder, and the malevolent influence is thus dissipated.

Among the Arabs the horn amulet is believed to render inert the malign glance of an enemy, and in the oases of the desert the horned heads of cattle are to be seen over the doors of the Arab dwellings as talismans.

In Lesbos the skulls of oxen or other horned creatures are fixed upon trees or sticks to avert the evil eye from the crops and fruits.

In Mongolia the horns of antelopes are prized on account of their alleged magical properties; fortune tellers and diviners affect to derive a knowledge of futurity by observation of the rings which encircle them. The Mongols set a high value upon whip handles made from these horns, and aver that their use by horsemen promotes endurance in their steeds.

———————❖··❖———————

Inasmuch as the horns of animals serve as weapons both for attack and defense, they were early associated in men's minds with the idea of power. Thus in ancient times the corners of altars were fashioned in the shape of horns, doubtless in order to symbolize the majesty and power of the Being in whose honor sacrifices were offered.

A propos of horns as symbols of strength, the peasants of Bannu, a district of the Punjab, believe that God placed the newly created world upon a cow's horn, the cow on a fish's back, and the fish on a stone; but what the stone rests upon, they do not venture to surmise. According to their theory, whenever the cow shakes her head, an earthquake naturally results.

———————❖··❖———————

The Siamese attribute therapeutic qualities to the horns and tusks of certain animals, and their pharmacopoeia contains a somewhat complex prescription used as a febrifuge, whose principal ingredients are the powdered horns of a rhinoceros, bison, and stag, the tusks of an elephant and tiger, and the teeth of a bear and crocodile. These are mixed together with water, and half of the resulting compound is to be swallowed, the remainder to be rubbed upon the body.

———————❖··❖———————

The *mano cornuta* or anti-witch gesture is used very generally in southern and central Italy. Its antiquity is vouched for by its representation in ancient paintings unearthed at Pompeii. It consists in flexing the two middle fingers, while the others are extended in imitation of horns. When the hand in this position is pointed at an obnoxious individual, the malignity of his glance is believed to be rendered inert.

---

In F. Marion Crawford's novel, *Pietro Ghisleri*, one of the characters, Laura Arden, was regarded in Roman society as a *jettatrice*, that is, one having the evil eye. Such a reputation once fastened on a person involves social ostracism. In the presence of the unfortunate individual every hand was hidden to make the talismanic gesture, and at the mere mention of her name all Rome 'made horns'. No one ever accosted her without having the fingers flexed in the approved fashion, unless, indeed, they had about them some potent amulet.

It is a curious fact that the possession of the evil eye may be imputed to anyone, regardless of character or position. Pope Pius IX was believed to have this malevolent power, and many devout Christians, while on their knees awaiting his benediction, were accustomed slyly to extend a hand toward him in the above-mentioned position.

---

In an article on 'Asiatic Symbolism' in the *Indian Antiquary*, Mr H.G.M. Murray-Aynsley says, in regard to Neapolitan evil-eye amulets, that they were probably introduced in southern Italy by Greek colonists of Asiatic ancestry, who settled at Cumae and other places in that neighborhood. Whether fashioned in the shape of horns or crescents, they are survivals of an ancient Chaldean symbol. It has been said that nothing, unless perhaps a superstitious belief, is more easily transmissible than a symbol; and the people of antiquity were wont to attribute to every symbol a talismanic value.

The modern Greeks, as well as the Italians, wear little charms representing the hand as making this gesture.

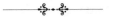

But not alone in the south of Europe exists the belief in the peculiar virtues of two-pronged objects, for in Norway reindeer horns are placed over the doors of farm buildings to drive off demons; and the fine antlers which grace the homes of successful hunters in our own country are doubtless often regarded by their owners as of more value than mere trophies of the chase, inasmuch as traditional fancy invests them with such extraordinary virtues.

In France a piece of stag horn is thought to be a preservative against witchcraft and disease, while in Portugal ox horns fastened on poles are placed in melon patches to protect the fruit from withering glances.

Among the Ossetes, a tribe of the Caucasus, the women arrange their hair in the shape of a chamois horn, curving forwards over the brow, thus forming a talismanic coiffure; and when a Muslim man takes his child on a journey he paints a crescent between its eyes, or tattooes the same device on its body. The modern Greek, too, adopts the precaution of attaching a crab's claw to the child's head. In northern Africa the horns of animals are very generally used as amulets, the prevailing idea being everywhere the same, namely, that pronged objects repel demons and evil glances.

---

Horns are used in eastern countries as ornaments to head-dresses, and serve, moreover, as symbols of rank. They are often made of precious metals, sometimes of wood. The *tantura*, worn by the Druses of Mount Lebanon in Syria, has this shape.

---

In the Bulgarian villages of Macedonia and Thrace the so-called wise woman, who combines the professions of witch and midwife, is an important character. Immediately upon the birth of a child this personage places a reaping hook in a corner of the room to keep away unfriendly spirits; the efficacy of the talisman being doubtless due partly to its shape, which bears considerable resemblance to a horseshoe.

---

And in Albania, a sickle, with which straw has just been cut, is placed for a few seconds on the stomach of a newly born child to prevent the demons who cause colic from exercising their functions.

---

The mystic virtue of the forked shape is not, however, restricted to its faculty of averting the glance of an evil eye or other malign influences, for the Divining Rod is believed to derive from this same peculiarity of form its magical power of detecting the presence of water or metals when wielded by an experienced hand.

———— ❧ ❧ ————

# THE SYMBOL
# OF THE OPEN HAND

It is worthy of note that the symbol of an open hand with extended fingers was a favorite talisman in former ages, and was to be seen, for example, at the entrances of dwellings in ancient Carthage. It is also found on Lybian and Phoenician tombs, as well as on Celtic monuments in French Brittany. Dr H.C. Trumbull quotes evidence from various writers showing that this symbol is in common use at the present time in several Eastern lands. In the region of ancient Babylonia the figure of a red outstretched hand is still displayed on houses and animals; and in Jerusalem the same token is frequently placed above the door or on the lintel on account of its reputed virtues in averting evil glances. The Spanish Jews of Jerusalem draw the figure of a hand in red upon the doors of their houses; and they also place upon their children's heads silver hand-shaped charms, which they believe to be specially obnoxious to unfriendly individuals desirous of bringing evil either upon the children themselves, or upon other members of the household.

———— ❧ ❧ ————

In different parts of Palestine the open-hand symbol appears alike on the houses of Christians, Jews and Muslims, usually painted in blue on or above the door. Claude Reignier

Conder, R.E., in *Heth and Moab*, remarks on the antiquity of this pagan emblem, which appears on Roman standards and on the sceptre of Siva in India. He is of the opinion that the figure of the red hand, whether sculptured on Irish crosses, displayed in Indian temples, or on Mexican buildings, is always an example of the same original idea – that of a protective symbol.

———————❖❖———————

A white handprint is commonly seen upon the doors and shutters of Jewish and Muslim houses in Beirut and other Syrian towns; and even the Christian residents of these towns sometimes mark windows and flour boxes with this emblem, after dipping the hand in whitewash, in order to 'avert chilling February winds from old people and to bring luck to the bin'.

———————❖❖———————

In Germany a rude amulet having the form of an open hand is fashioned out of the stems of coarse plants, and is deemed an ample safeguard against divers misfortunes and sorceries. It is called 'the hand of Saint John', or 'the hand of Fortune'.

———————❖❖———————

The Jewish matrons of Algeria fasten little golden hands to their children's caps, or to their glass-bead necklaces, and they themselves carry about similar luck tokens.

———————❖❖———————

In north-western Scotland whoever enters a house where butter is being made is expected to lay his hand upon the churn, thereby signifying that he has no evil designs against the butter-maker, and dissipating any possible effects of an evil eye. As a charm against malevolent influences, the Arabs of Algeria make use of rude drawings representing an open hand, placed either above the entrances of their habitations or within doors – a symbolical translation of the well-known Arabic imprecation, 'Five fingers in thine eye!' Oftentimes the same meaning is conveyed by five lines, one shorter than the others to indicate the thumb.

---

# CRESCENTS AND HALF-MOON-SHAPED AMULETS

The alleged predominant influence of the moon's wax and wane over the growth and welfare of vegetation was formerly generally recognized. Thus in an almanac of the year 1661 it is stated that:

> If any corn, seed, or plant be either set or sown within six hours either before or after the full Moon in Summer, or before the new Moon in Winter, having joined with the cosmical rising of Arcturus and Orion, the Haedi and the Sicidi, it is subject to blasting and canker.

---

Timber was always cut during the wane of the moon, and so firmly rooted was this superstition that directions were given accordingly in the Forest Code of France.

An early English almanac advised farmers to kill hogs when
the moon was growing, as thus 'the bacon would prove the
better in boiling'.

Moon-worship was one of the most ancient forms of idolatry,
and still exists among some Eastern nations. A relic of the
practice is seen in some parts of Great Britain in the custom
of bowing to the new moon.

Astrologers regarded the moon as exerting a powerful
influence over the health and fortunes of human beings,
according to her aspect and position at the time of their birth.
Thus in a *Manual of Astrology* by Raphael, she is described as
a 'cold, moist, watery, phlegmatic planet, and partaking of
good or evil as she is aspected by good or evil stars'.

The growing horned moon was thought to exert a mysterious
beneficent influence not only over many of the operations of agriculture, but over the affairs of everyday life as
well. Hence doubtless arose the belief in the value of crescent-shaped and cornute objects as amulets and charms; of
these the horseshoe is the one most commonly available, and
therefore the one most generally used.

In astrology the moon has indeed always been considered the most influential of the heavenly bodies by reason of her rapid motion and nearness to the earth; and the astrologers of old, whether in forecasting future events or in giving advice as to proper times and seasons for the transaction of business affairs, first ascertained whether or not the moon were well aspected. This was also a cardinal point with the shrewd magicians of later centuries. And should anyone require proof of the existence of a modern belief in lunar influences, let him consult Zadkiel's *Almanac* for the year 1898. Therein he will find it stated that when the sun is in benefic aspect with the moon, it is a suitable day for asking favors, seeking employment, and traveling for health.

Venus in benefic aspect with the moon is favorable for courting, marrying, visiting friends, engaging maid-servants, and seeking amusement.

Mars, for consulting surgeons and dealing with engineers and soldiers.

Jupiter, for opening offices and places of business, and for beginning new enterprises.

Saturn, for having to do with farmers, miners, and elderly people, for buying real estate and for planting and sowing.

For, says the oracle of the almanac, astrologers have found by experience that if the above instructions are followed, human affairs proceed smoothly.

———————❧ ❧———————

In his work entitled *The Evil-Eye*, Mr Frederick Thomas Elworthy calls attention to the fact that the half-moon was often placed on the heads of certain of the most powerful Egyptian deities, and therefore when worn became a symbol of their worship. Indeed, the crescent is common in the religious symbolism not only of ancient Egypt, but also of Assyria and India. The Hebrew maidens in the time of the prophet Isaiah wore crescent-shaped ornaments on their heads.

---

The crescent is the well-known symbol of the Turkish religion. According to tradition, Philip of Macedon, the father of Alexander the Great, attempted to undermine the walls of Byzantium during a siege of the city, but the attempt was revealed to the inhabitants by the light of a crescent moon. Whereupon they erected a statue to Diana, and adopted the crescent as their symbol.

When the Byzantine empire was overthrown by Mohammed II, in 1453, the Turks regarded the crescent, which was everywhere to be seen, as of favorable import. They therefore made it their own emblem, and it has since continued to be a distinctively Mohammedan token.

---

Golden crescents of various sizes were among the most primitive forms of money. Ancient coins frequently bore the likenesses of popular deities or their symbols, and of the latter the crescent appears to have been the one most commonly employed. It was the usual mint-mark of the coins of Thespia in the early part of the fourth century BC; is seen on the coins of the reigns of Augustus, Nero, and other Roman emperors; and on the silver pieces of the time of Hadrian is found the *Luna crescens* with seven stars.

---

A crescent adorned the head of the goddess Diana in her character of Hecate, or ruler of the infernal regions. Hecate was supposed to preside over enchantments, and was also the special guardian and protectress of houses and doors. The Greeks not only wore amulets in the shape of the half moon, but placed them on the walls of their houses as talismans; and the Romans used *phalerae*, metallic disks and crescents, to decorate the foreheads and breasts of their horses.

Such ornaments are to be seen on the caparisons of the horses on Trajan's Column and on other ancient monuments, in the collection of Roman antiquities in the British Museum, and in mediaeval paintings and tapestries.

In the portrayals of combats between the Romans and Dacians on the Arch of Constantine, the trappings of the horses of both armies are decorated with these emblems, as are also the bridle reins of a horse shown in a French manuscript of the fifteenth century representing 'gentlefolk meeting on horseback'.

Charms of similar shape, made of wolves' teeth and boars' tusks, have been found in tumuli in different parts of Great Britain.

A sepulchral stone, which is preserved among other Gallo-Roman relics within the Chateau of Chinon, France, bears the effigy of a man standing upright and clad in a large tunic with wide sleeves. Above the figure is a crescent-shaped talisman, a symbol frequently found in monuments of that period.

But the use of these symbols, although so ancient, is by no means obsolete; the brass crescent, an avowed charm against the evil eye, is very commonly attached to the elaborately decorated harnesses of Neapolitan draught horses, and is used in the East to embellish the trappings of elephants. It is also still employed in like manner in various parts of Europe and in the England of today.

In Germany small half-moon-shaped amulets similar to the ancient *μηνισχιο* or *lunulae* are still used against the evil eye.

In Sweden and Frisia, bridal ornaments for the head and neck often represent the moon's disk in its first quarter; and it is customary to call out after a newly married pair, 'Increase, Moon'.

Elworthy remarks that the horseshoe, wherever used as an amulet, is the handy conventional representative of the crescent, and that the Buddhist crescent emblem is a horseshoe with the curve pointed like a Gothic arch.

The English fern called moonwort is thought to owe its reputed magical powers to the crescent form of the segments of its frond. Some writers regard it as identical with the martagon, an herb formerly much used by sorcerers; and also with the Italian *sferracavallo*.

According to the famous astrologer and herbalist, Nicholas Culpeper, moonwort possessed certain occult virtues, and was endowed with extraordinary attributes, chief among them being its power of undoing locks and of unshoeing horses. The same writer remarked that, while some people of intelligence regarded these notions with scorn, the popular name for moonwort among the countryfolk was 'unshoe-the-horse'.

The horseshoe has sometimes been identified with the cross, and has been supposed to derive its amuletic power from a fancied resemblance to the sacred Christian symbol. But inasmuch as it is difficult to find any marked similarity in form between the crescent and the cross, this theory does not appear to warrant serious consideration.

# IRON AS A
## PROTECTIVE CHARM

Some writers have maintained that the luck associated with the horseshoe is due chiefly to the metal, irrespective of its shape, as iron and steel are traditional charms against malevolent spirits and goblins. In their view, a horseshoe is simply a piece of iron of graceful shape and convenient form, commonly pierced with seven nail-holes (a mystic number), and therefore an altogether suitable talisman to be affixed to the door of dwelling or stable in conformity with a venerable custom sanctioned by centuries of usage. Of the antiquity of the belief in the supernatural properties of iron there can be no doubt.

Among the ancient Gauls this metal was thought to be consecrated to the Evil Principle, and, according to a fragment of the writings of the Egyptian historian Manetho (about 275 BC), iron was called in Egypt the bone of Typhon, or Devil's bone, for Typhon in the Egyptian mythology was the personification of evil.

Pliny, in his *Natural History*, states that iron coffin nails affixed to the lintel of the door render the inmates of the dwelling secure from the visitations of nocturnal prowling spirits.

According to the same author, iron has valuable attributes as a preservative against harmful witchcrafts and sorceries, and may thus be used with advantage both by adults and children. For this purpose it was only necessary to trace a circle about one's self with a piece of the metal, or thrice to swing a sword around one's body. Moreover, gentle proddings with a sword wherewith a man has been wounded were reputed to alleviate divers aches and pains, and even iron-rust had its own healing powers: 'If a horse be shod with shoes made from a sword wherewith a man has been slain, he will be most swift and fleet, and never, though never so hard rode, tire.'

---

A young herdswoman was once tending cattle in a forest of Vermaland in Sweden; and the weather being cold and wet, she carried along her tinder-box with flint and steel, as is customary in that country. Presently along came a giantess carrying a casket, which she asked the girl to keep while she went away to invite some friends to attend her daughter's marriage.

Quite thoughtlessly the girl laid her fire-steel on the casket, and when the giantess returned for the property she could not touch it, for steel is repellant to trolls, both great and small. So the herdswoman carried home the treasure box, which was found to contain a golden crown and other valuables.

---

The heathen Northmen believed in the existence of a race of dwarfish artisans, who were skilled in the working of metals, and who fashioned implements of warfare in their subterranean workshops. These dwarfs were also thought to inhabit isolated rocks; and according to a popular notion, if a man chanced to encounter one of them, and quickly threw a piece of steel between him and his habitation, he could thereby prevent the dwarf from returning home, and could exact of him whatever he desired.

———— ❧··❧ ————

Among French Canadians, fireflies are viewed with superstitious eyes as luminous imps of evil, and iron and steel are the most potent safeguards against them; a knife or needle stuck into the nearest fence is thought to amply protect the belated wayfarer against these insects, for they will either do themselves injury upon the former, or will become so exhausted in endeavoring to pass through the needle's eye as to render them temporarily harmless. Such waifs and strays of popular credulity may seem most trivial, yet they serve to illustrate the ancient and widely diffused belief in the traditional qualities ascribed to certain metals.

———— ❧··❧ ————

One widely prevalent theory ascribed to iron a meteoric origin, but the different nations of antiquity were wont to attribute its discovery or invention to some favorite deity or mythological personage; Osiris was thus honored by the Egyptians, Vulcan by the Romans, and Wodan or Odin by the Teutons.

———— ❧··❧ ————

In early times the employment of iron in the arts was much restricted by reason of its dull exterior and brittleness. There existed, moreover, among the Romans a certain religious prejudice against the metal, whose use in many ceremonies was wholly proscribed.

This prejudice appears to have been due to the fact that iron weapons were held jointly responsible with those who wielded them for the shedding of human blood; inasmuch as swords, knives, battle axes, lance and spear points, and other implements of war were made of iron.

———— ❧ • ❧ ————

Those mythical demons of Oriental lands known as the Jinn are believed to be exorcised by the mere name of iron; and Arabs when overtaken by a simoom in the desert endeavor to charm away these spirits of evil by crying, 'Iron, iron!'

The Jinn being legendary creatures of the Stone Age, the comparatively modern metal is supposed to be obnoxious to them. In Scandinavia and in northern countries generally, iron is a historic charm against the wiles of sorcerers.

———— ❧ • ❧ ————

The Chinese sometimes wear outside of their clothing a piece of an old iron plough-point as a charm; and they have also a custom of driving long iron nails in certain kinds of trees to exorcise some particularly dangerous female demons which haunt them. The ancient Irish were wont to hang crooked horseshoe nails about the necks of their children as charms; and in Teutonic folklore we find the venerable superstition that a horseshoe nail found by chance and driven into the fireplace will effect the restoration of stolen property to the owner. In Ireland, at the present time, iron is held to be a sacred and luck-bringing metal which thieves hesitate to steal.

A Celtic legend says that the name *Iron-land* or *Ireland* originated as follows. The Emerald Isle was formerly altogether submerged, except during a brief period every seventh year, and at such times repeated attempts were made by foreigners to land on its soil, but without success, as the advancing waves always swallowed up the bold invaders. Finally a heavenly revelation declared that the island could only be rescued from the sea by throwing a piece of iron upon it during its brief appearance above the waters. Profiting by the information thus vouchsafed, a daring adventurer cast his sword upon the land at the time indicated, thereby dissolving the spell, and Ireland has ever since remained above the water. On account of this tradition the finding of iron is always accounted lucky by the Irish; and when the treasure trove has the form of a horseshoe, it is nailed up over the house door. Thus iron is believed to have reclaimed Ireland from the sea, and the talismanic symbol of its reclamation is the iron horseshoe.

Once upon a time – so runs a tradition of the Ukraine, the border region between Russia and Poland – some men found a piece of iron. After having in vain attempted to eat it, they tried to soften it by boiling it in water; then they roasted it, and afterwards beat it with stones. While thus engaged, the Devil, who had been watching them, inquired, 'What are you making there?' and the men replied, 'A hammer with which to beat the Devil.' Thereupon Satan asked where they had obtained the requisite sand; and from that time men understood that sand was essential for the use of iron workers; and thus began the manufacture of iron implements.

---

Among the Scotch fishermen also iron is invested with magical attributes. Thus if, when plying their vocation, one of their number chance to indulge in profanity, the others at once call out, 'Cauld airn!' and each grasps a handy piece of the metal as a counter influence to the misfortune which would else pursue them throughout the day. Even nowadays in England, in default of a horseshoe, the iron plates of the heavy shoes worn by farm laborers are occasionally to be seen fastened at the doors of their cottages.

---

When in former times a belief in the existence of mischievous elves was current in the Highland districts of Scotland, iron and steel were in high repute as popular safeguards against the visits of these fairy folk; for they were sometimes bold enough to carry off young mothers, whom they compelled to act as wet nurses for their own offspring. One evening many years ago a farmer named Ewen Macdonald, of Duldreggan, left his wife and young infant indoors while he went out on an errand; and tradition has it that while crossing a brook, thereafter called in the Gaelic tongue 'the streamlet of the knife', he heard a strange rushing sound accompanied with a sigh, and realized at once that fairies were carrying off his wife. Instantly throwing a knife into the air in the name of the Trinity, the fairies' power was annulled, and his wife dropped down before him.

---

In Scandinavian and Scottish folklore, there is a marked affinity between iron and flint. The elf-bolt or flint arrowhead was formerly in great repute as a charm against divers evil influences, whether carried around as an amulet, used as a magical purifier of drinking water for cattle, or to avert fairy spite. It seems possible that iron and steel in superseding flint, which was so useful a material in the rude arts of primitive peoples, inherited its ancient magical qualities.

———— ❧ ❦ ————

In the Hebrides a popular charm against the wiles of sorcerers consisted in placing pieces of flint and untempered steel in the milk of cows alleged to have been bewitched. The milk was then boiled, and this process was thought to foil the machinations of the witch or enchantress. The fairies of the Scottish lowlands were supposed to use arrows tipped with white flint, wherewith they shot the cattle of persons obnoxious to them, the wounds thus inflicted being invisible except to certain personages gifted with supernatural sight.

———— ❧ ❦ ————

According to a Cornish belief, iron is potent to control the water-fiends, and when thrown overboard enables mariners to land on a rocky coast with safety even in a rough sea. A similar superstition exists in the Orkney Islands with reference to a certain rock on the coast of Westray. It is thought that when anyone with a piece of iron about him steps upon this rock, the sea at once becomes turbulent and does not subside until the magical substance is thrown into the water.

———— ❧ ❦ ————

The inhabitants of the rocky island of Timor, in the Indian Archipelago, carry about them scraps of iron to preserve themselves from all kinds of mishaps, even as the London cockney cherishes with care his lucky penny, crooked sixpence, or perforated shilling; while in Hindustan iron nails are frequently driven in over a door, or into the legs of a bedstead, as protectives. It was a medieval wedding custom in France to place on the bride's finger a ring made from a horseshoe nail, a superstitious bid, as it were, for happy auspices.

In Sicily, iron amulets are popularly used against the evil eye; indeed iron in any form, especially the horseshoe, is thought to be effective, and in fact talismanic properties are ascribed to all metals. When, therefore, a Sicilian feels that he is being 'overlooked', he instantly touches the first available metallic object, such as his watch chain, keys, or coins.

Wherever, therefore, such notions exist, talismans are naturally employed to render inert the machinations of these little demons; and of all these safeguards, iron and steel are perhaps the most potent. Quite commonly in Germany, among the lower classes, such articles as knives, hatchets, and cutting instruments generally, as well as fire-irons, harrows, keys and needles, are considered protectives against disease if placed near or about the sick person.

In Morocco it is customary to place a dagger under the patient's pillow, and in Greece a black-handled knife is similarly used to keep away the nightmare.

In Germany iron implements laid crosswise are considered to be powerful anti-witch safeguards for infants; and in Switzerland two knives, or a knife and fork, are placed in the cradle under the pillow. In Bohemia a knife on which a cross is marked, and in Bavaria a pair of opened scissors, are similarly used. In Westphalia an axe and a broom are laid crosswise on the threshold, the child's nurse being expected to step over these articles on entering the room.

The therapeutic value of iron and its use as a medicament do not properly belong to our subject; and, indeed, neither the iron horseshoe nor its counterfeit symbol have usually been much employed in folk medicine. Professor Sepp, in his work on the religion of the early Germans, mentions, however, a popular cure for whooping cough, which consisted in having the patient eat off of a wooden platter branded with the figure of a horseshoe.

In France, also, a favorite panacea for children's diseases consists in laying on the child an accidentally found horseshoe, with the nails remaining in it; and in Mecklenburg gastric affections are thought to be successfully treated by drinking beer which has been poured upon a red-hot horseshoe.

Pliny ascribed healing power to a cast-off horseshoe found on the road. The finder was recommended carefully to preserve such a horseshoe; and should he at any future time be afflicted with the hiccoughs, the mere recollection of the exact spot where the shoe had been placed would serve as a remedy for that sometimes obstinate affection.

———————————— ❧ • ❧ ————————————

In Bavaria a popular alleged cure for hernia in children is as follows: from a horseshoe wherein all the nails remain, and which has been cast by a horse, a nail is taken; and when next a new moon comes on a Friday, one must go into a field or orchard before sunrise and drive the nail by three blows into an oak tree or pear tree, according to the sex of the child, and thrice invoke the name of Christ; after which one must kneel on the ground in front of the tree and repeat a Paternoster. This is an example of a kind of therapeutic measure not uncommon among peasants in different parts of Germany, a blending of the use of a superstitious charm with religious exercises.

———————————— ❧ • ❧ ————————————

An ingenious theory ascribes the origin of the belief in the magical properties of iron to the early employment of the actual cautery, and to the use of the lancet in surgery. In either case the healing effects of the metal, whether hot or in the form of a knife, have been attributed by superstitious minds to magical properties in the instruments, whereby the demons who caused the disease were put to flight. In northern India the natives believe that evil spirits are so simple minded as to run against the sharp edge of a knife and thus do themselves injury; and they also make use of iron rings as demon scarers, such talismans having the double efficacy of the iron and of the sacred circle.

———————❧••❧———————

In Bombay, when a child is born, the natives place an iron bar along the threshold of the room of confinement as a guard against the entrance of demons. This practice is derived from the Hindu superstition that evil spirits keep aloof from iron; and even today pieces of horseshoes are to be seen nailed to the bottom sills of the doors of native houses.

———————❧••❧———————

In east Bothnia, when the cows leave their winter quarters for the first time, an iron bar is laid before the threshold of the door through which the animals must pass, and the farmers believe that, if this precaution were omitted, the cows would prove troublesome throughout the summer. So, too, in the region of Saalfield, in central Germany, it is customary to place axes, saws, and other iron and steel implements outside the stable door to keep the cattle from bewitchment.

———————❧••❧———————

The Scandinavian peasants, when they venture upon the water, are wont to protect themselves against the power of the *Neck*, or river-spirit, by placing a knife in the bottom of the boat, or by fixing an iron nail in a reed. The following is the translation of a charm used in Norway for this purpose: 'Neck, Neck, nail in water, the Virgin Mary casteth steel in water. Do you sink, I flit.'

In Finland there is an evil fairy known as the Alp Nightmare. Its name in the vernacular is *Painajainen*, which means in English 'Presser'. This unpleasant being makes people scream, and causes young children to squint; and the popular safeguard is steel, or a broom placed beneath the pillow.

Among the Jews there prevails a popular belief that one should never make use of a knife or other steel instrument for the purpose of more readily following with the eye the pages of the Bible, the Talmud, or other sacred book. Iron should never be permitted to touch any book treating of religion, for the two are incompatible by nature, the one destroying human life and the other prolonging it. The Highlanders of Scotland have a time-honored custom of taking an oath upon cold iron or steel. The dirk, which was formerly an indispensable adjunct to the Highland costume, is a favorite and handy object for the purpose. The faith in the magical power of steel and iron against evil-disposed fairies and ghosts was universal, and this form of oath was more solemn and binding than any other.

Among the Bavarian peasants nails and needles have a reputation the reverse of that of the horseshoe. A horseshoe nail stuck into the front door of a house will give the owner a serious illness. A needle, when given to a friend, is sure to prick to death existing friendship, even as such friendship is severed by the gift of a knife or pair of scissors. Such an untoward result may be averted, however, if the recipient smile pleasantly when the gift is made. A curious superstition about iron locks prevails in Styria and Tyrol. If you procure from a locksmith a brand-new lock and carry it to church at the time of a wedding ceremony, and if, while the benediction is being said, you fasten the lock by a turn of the key, then the young couple's love and happiness is destroyed. Mutual aversion will supplant affection until you open the lock again.

# FIRE AS A
# SPIRIT-SCARING ELEMENT

The horseshoe is a product of the artisan's skill by the aid of fire.

This element has in all ages been considered the great purifier, and a powerful foe to evil spirits.

The Chaldeans venerated fire and esteemed it a deity, and among primitive nations everywhere it has ever been held sacred. The Persians had fire temples, called Pyrcea, devoted solely to the preservation of the holy fire.

In the *Rig-Veda*, the principal sacred book of the Hindus, the crackling of burning fagots was listened to as the voice of the gods, and the same superstition prevails still among the natives of Borneo.

---

In a fragment of the writings of Menander Protector, a Greek historian of the sixth century, it is related that when an embassy sent by the Emperor Justin reached Sogdiana, the ancient Bokhara, it was met by a party of Turks, who proceeded to exorcise their baggage by beating drums and ringing bells over it. They then ran around the baggage, bearing aloft flaming leaves, meantime, by their gestures and movements, seeking to repel evil spirits; after which some of the party themselves passed through fire as a means of purification.

---

Fire is especially potent against nocturnal demons, and also against the evil spirits which cause disease in cattle. Hence the utility of the ancient 'need-fires', produced by the friction of two pieces of wood, which were thought to be an antidote against the murrain and epizootics generally – a custom until recently in vogue in the Scottish Highlands, and formerly practiced in many other regions.

---

The midsummer fires kindled on Saint John's Eve, in accordance with an ancient British custom, were regarded as purifiers of the air. Moreover, the whole area of ground illuminated by these fires was reckoned to be freed from sorcery for a year, and, by leaping through the flames, both men and cattle were insured safety against demons for a like period.

———⁂———

In Ireland it was customary for people to run through the streets on Saint John's Eve carrying long poles, upon which were tied flaming bundles of straw, in order to purify the air, for at that time all kinds of mischievous imps, hobgoblins, and devils were abroad, intent on working injury to human beings.

———⁂———

Midsummer fires were still lighted in Ireland in the latter half of the nineteenth century, a survival of pagan fire-worship. In many countries people gathered about the bonfires, while children leaped through the flames, and live coals were carried into the cornfields as an antidote to blight.

Sometimes the remaining ashes were scattered over the neighboring fields, in order to protect the crops from ravaging vermin or insects; and in Sweden the smoke of need-fires was reputed to stimulate the growth of fruit-trees, and to impart luck to fishing nets hung up in it.

———⁂———

When a child is born, the Hindus light fires to frighten demons; and for the same reason lamps are swung to and fro at weddings, and fire is carried before the dead body at a funeral.

———⁂———

Devout Brahmins keep a fire constantly burning in their houses and worship it daily, expecting thereby to secure for themselves good fortune. The origin of the respect accorded to fire among these people has been attributed to its potency in alleviating or curing certain diseases, as, for example, when applied in the actual cautery, or by means of the *moxa*; for, wherever a belief exists in demoniacal possession as the cause of bodily disorders, the cure of the latter is evidence that the malignant spirits have been put to flight.

---

The fire-worshiping Parsees also keep a fire continuously in the lying-in room; and when a child is ailing from any cause, they fasten to its left arm a magical charm of written words prepared by a priest, exorcising the evil spirits in the name of their chief deity, Ormuzd, and 'binding them by the power and beauty of fire'.

---

On the birth of a child among the Khoikhoi of South Africa a household fire is kindled, which is maintained until the healing of the child's navel; and when a member of the tribe goes a-hunting, his wife is careful to keep a fire burning indoors; for, if it were allowed to go out, the husband would have no luck.

---

## THE SERPENTINE SHAPE OF THE HORSESHOE

The theory has been advanced that in ancient idolatrous times the horseshoe in its primitive form was a symbol in serpent worship, and that its superstitious use as a charm may have thus originated. This seems plausible enough, inasmuch as there is a resemblance between the horseshoe and the arched body of the snake, when the latter is so convoluted that its head and tail correspond to the horseshoe prongs.

Both snakes and horseshoes were anciently engraved on stones and medals, presumably as amuletic symbols; and in front of a church in Crendi, a town in the southern part of the island of Malta, there is to be seen a statue having at its feet a protective symbol in the shape of a half moon encircled by a snake.

The serpent played an important role in Asiatic and ancient Egyptian symbolism. This has been thought to be due partly to a belief that the sun's path through the heavens formed a serpentine curve, and partly because lightning, or the fertilizing fire, sometimes flashes upon the earth in a snake-like zigzag. The serpent was endowed with the attributes of divinity on account of its graceful and easy movements, the brightness of its eyes, the function of discarding its skin (a process which was regarded as emblematic of a renewal of its youth), and its instantaneous spring upon its prey. The worship of serpents is of great antiquity, the earliest authentic accounts of the custom being found in Chaldean and Chinese astronomical works. It was nearly universal among the most ancient nations of the world, and this universality has been ascribed to the traditionary remembrance of the serpent in Eden, and has given rise to the opinion of some writers that snake-worship may have been the primitive religion of the human race.

———————❖••❖———————

On the walls of houses in Pompeii are to be seen the figures of
snakes, which are believed to have been intended as preservative symbols; and we learn from Mr C.G. Leland's 'Etruscan
Roman Remains' that the peasants of the mountainous
regions in northern Italy, known as the Romagna Toscana,
have a custom of painting on the walls of their houses the
figures of serpents with the heads and tails pointing upward.
These are intended both as amulets to keep away witches, and
as luck-bringers, and are therefore exact counterparts of the
horseshoe and the crescent as magical emblems.

The more interlaced the snake's coils, the more effective
the amulet; the idea being that a witch is obliged to trace out
and follow with her eye the interweaving convolutions, and
that in attempting to do this she becomes bewildered, and is
temporarily rendered incapable of doing harm.

———————❖••❖———————

In ancient Roman works of art the serpent is sometimes
portrayed as a protective symbol. In some bronze figures of
Fortune unearthed at Herculaneum, serpents are represented
either as encircling the arm of the goddess, or as entwined
about her cornucopia, thus typifying, as it were, the idea of
the intimate association of the snake with good luck.

———————❖••❖———————

The Phoenicians rendered homage to serpents, and history
shows that the Lithuanians, Sarmatians, or inhabitants of
ancient Poland, and other nations of central Europe, treated

these reptiles with superstitious respect. In Russia, also, domestic snakes were formerly carefully nurtured, for they were thought to bring good fortune to the members of a household.

The worship of serpents is still practiced in Persia, Tibet, Ceylon, and other Eastern lands. In western Africa, also, the serpent is a chief deity, and is appealed to by the natives in seasons of drought and pestilence.

A talisman having the form of a snake, and known as *la sirena*, is in use among the lower classes at Naples.

In the folklore of the south Slavonian nations the serpent is regarded as a protective genius, not only of the people, but of domestic animals and houses as well. Every human being has a snake as tutelary divinity, with which his growth and well-being are closely connected, and the killing of one of these sacred creatures was formerly deemed a grave offense. To meet with a snake has long been accounted fortunate in some countries. The south Slav peasant believes that whoever encounters one of these creatures, on first going into the woods in the spring, will be prosperous throughout the year. But on the other hand he regards it as an evil omen if he happens to catch a glimpse of his own tutelary serpent. Fortunately, however, a man never knows which particular ophidian is his special guardian.

———— ❖ • ❖ ————

The relation of the serpent to sculptured or engraved stones reveals to us the reptile as still the object of veneration, if not of adoration, among widely remote nations. If we search among the tombs of Egypt, Assyria, and Etruria, we shall find innumerable signets, cylinders, and *scarabei* of gems engraved with serpents; these were proverbially worn as amulets, or used as insignia of authority; and, in the temples and tombs of these and other countries, serpents are engraved or sculptured or painted, either as hieroglyphics or as forming symbolical ornaments of deities or genii. In India they are sculptured twining around all the gods of the cave temples which mark the graves of kings and heroes, and the oldest of the Scandinavian runes are written within the folds of serpents engraved on stones.

———— ❖ • ❖ ————

In ancient Mexican temples the serpent symbol is frequently seen. The approach to the temple of El Castillo, at Chichen in Yucatan, is guarded by a pair of huge serpent heads, and a second pair protect the entrance to the sanctuary. Figures of serpents also appear in the Mosaic relief designs of the facades, and within on the sanctuary walls. So, too, in the temples of Palenque and other southern Mexican towns, serpents are everywhere plentiful in the decorations and sculptures.

Representations of snakes are to be seen on the walls of houses in many parts of India at the present day, and villages have their special ophite guardians.

———— ❖ • ❖ ————

The fifth day of the first or bright half of the lunar month S'ravana, which nearly corresponds with August, is celebrated by the Brahmins in honor of the *naga* or cobra. Some interesting details of the ceremonies on these occasions are given in Balfour's *Cyclopaedia of India*. We learn from this source that native women are wont at such times to join in dancing around snake-holes, and also to prostrate themselves and invoke blessings; while others bow down before living cobras at their own homes, or worship figures of serpents.

———————✣··✣———————

Visits from snakes are highly appreciated as auspicious events, and the reptiles are sure of a hospitable reception, because they are looked upon as tutelary divinities.

Thus the serpent was held sacred by the nations of antiquity, being a prominent feature in every mythology and symbolizing many pagan divinities.

———————✣··✣———————

The Vlach women of European Turkey, who inhabit villages in the mountain ranges of Thessaly and Albania, treat serpents with great respect and even with veneration. If one of the harmless white snakes which abound in the country chances to enter a cottage, it is provided with food and allowed to depart unharmed, its appearance indoors being accounted a lucky event. Such friendly treatment often results in the snake's becoming domesticated and receiving the title of 'house-serpent'. The Carinthians, too, are wont to treat snakes as fondlings, for they consider that these reptiles bring good luck proportionate in degree to their bodily diameter; hence they are fed with care and provided with bowls of milk twice a day.

Indeed, in many countries the serpent or dragon, originally a guardian of treasure, is considered a house-protector. The same conception is embodied in the grotesque dragon-headed gargoyles so common in medieval architecture.

Many derivatives from the Hebrew and Arabic words for serpent signify the practice of sorcery, consultation with familiar spirits, and intercourse with demons.

It would seem, therefore, not improbable that the horseshoe amulet has acquired some portion of the magical influences ascribed to it through its serpentine form.

## THE HORSESHOE AS A SYMBOL OF THE HORSE

An English myth ascribes to the horse the character of a luck-bringer, and horse-worship was in vogue among the early Celts, Teutons and Slavs.

In Hindustan, also, the horse is regarded as a lucky animal; and when an equestrian rides into a sugar-cane field in the sowing season, the event is considered auspicious. In the same region the froth from a horse's mouth is thought to repel demons, which are believed to have more fear of a horse than of any other animal. The natives of northern India also believe that the horse was originally a winged creature, and that the horny protuberances on his legs indicate where the wings were attached.

———— ❖ ❖ ————

In the Norse mythology almost every deity has his particular steed, as have most of the heroes of antiquity, for the heathen nations regarded the horse as sacred and divine.

———— ❖ ❖ ————

Tradition says that when the city of Carthage was founded by Dido, the Phoenician queen, in the ninth century BC, a priestess of Juno dug in the ground, by command of the oracle, and discovered the head of a bullock. This was considered unsatisfactory, because bullocks and oxen were servile animals under the yoke. Thereupon the priestess again turned up the soil and found a horse's head, which was reckoned auspicious, for the horse, although sometimes yoked to the plough, was also symbolic of war and martial glory. Therefore a temple of Juno was built on the spot, and the figure of a horse's head was adopted as an emblem by the Carthaginians and stamped upon their coins.

———— ❖ ❖ ————

Dr Ludwig Beck, in his *History of Iron*, states that in Teutonic legends the horse was sacred to Wodan or Odin, who always rode, while Thor either drove about in his chariot or went afoot. Thence it is, says this writer, that the Devil of the Middle Ages is represented with the hoofs of a horse.

———⁂———

The reputation of the horse as a prophetic and divinatory animal, even among Christian peoples, is shown by various German traditions, of which the following is an example. When the inhabitants of Delve, a village in the Duchy of Holstein, were about to build a church, the choice of a site was determined in this manner: an image of the Virgin was fastened upon the back of a parti-colored mare, which was then allowed to roam at will; and it was agreed that the church should be erected upon the spot where the mare should be found the next morning. This proved to be a neighboring bramble thicket, and the new edifice was accordingly placed there, and dedicated to 'Our beloved Lady on the Horse'.

———⁂———

The ancient belief in the oracular powers of the horse is well shown by a custom formerly in vogue among the Pomeranians. On the outbreak of a war a priest laid three spears at equal distances upon the ground in front of the temple. Two other spears were then leaned transversely across them, with their points resting in the earth. After a prayer the high priest led up a sacred horse, and if he stepped with his right foot foremost thrice in succession over the spears without stumbling, it was accounted a good augury, otherwise not.

———⁂———

A dragon-headed horse, emblematic of grandeur, having on its back the civilizing book of the law, is one of the four great mythic animals of the Chinese; and the Tibetans have a like symbol, which they use as a luck-bringing talisman.

The association of the horse with luck is prominent in Indian myth as well: the jewel-horse of the universal monarch, such as Buddha was to have been had he cared for worldly grandeur, carries its rider Pegasus-like through the air in whatever direction wished for, and thus it would become associated with the idea of material wishes, and especially wealth and jewels.

Among the lower classes of the Hindus of Bombay, a notion is prevalent that spirits are frightened by the sound of a horse's hoofs; and this superstition has been thought to explain the custom, in vogue among the Hindus generally, of having a bridegroom ride a horse when on his way to the bride's residence.

In Bokhara, when a horse stumbles in fording a stream, and the rider thereby gets an involuntary wetting, it is considered a most fortunate occurrence instead of a mishap. In the same country it is also accounted lucky to meet an equestrian.

One reason in favor of the theory which ascribes the horse-shoe's weird powers to its connection with a luck-bringing animal is the fact that various portions of the equine frame serve as amulets in different localities. Thus not only the horseshoe but the hoof, or even a single bone of the foot, may be used for this object.

---

In the island of Montserrat the two incisor teeth of a horse are carried about as charms. The popular belief of many people credits equine hair with special virtues. 'Honor abides in the manes of horses' is a saying of Mohammed, and in Turkey a horse's tail as an emblem is significant of dignity and exalted position.

---

In certain villages of Brandenburg every newborn boy, before his first bath, is placed upon a horse, the animal being brought into the chamber for the purpose. This is thought to impart to the child manly qualities for life. In other districts small children are allowed to ride a black foal to facilitate the cutting of their teeth; and the neighings of horses are believed to be of favorable import if listened to carefully. The popular belief on this subject is exemplified in the German saying, 'He has horse-luck', in reference to a piece of extraordinary good fortune.

---

The Irish think that the reason for the horseshoe's magical power is because the horse and the ass were in the stable where Christ was born, and hence are evermore blessed animals.

The romantic literature of Ireland affords evidence of the existence of a species of horse-worship in that country in former ages, and tradition says that in the olden time there were horses endowed with human faculties. We learn from Tacitus, moreover, that the Teutonic peoples used white horses, as the Romans used chickens, for purposes of augury, and divined future events from different intonations of neighings. Hence it probably is that the discovery of a horseshoe is so univer-sally thought lucky, some of the feelings that once attached to the animal itself still surviving around the iron of its hoof. For horses, like dogs and birds, were universally accredited with a greater insight into futurity than man himself.

---

The horse is seen among the insignia of Kent, the first of the Anglo-Saxon kingdoms, and is displayed at the present time on the shields of the houses of Hanover and Brunswick.

---

One of the most solemn forms of oath taken on the eve of battle required a warrior to swear 'by the shoulder of a horse and the edge of a sword' that he would not flee from the enemy even if the latter should be superior in strength.

---

At the time of the conquest of Peru, the Indian aborigines were amazed at the sight of the Spanish horsemen, believing that man and horse were one creature. And it is said that Pizarro owed his life to this superstitious belief; for on one occasion, when pursued by the natives, he fell from his horse, and the Peruvians who witnessed the mishap, believing that one animal had by magic divided itself into two, gave up the pursuit in dismay.

---

M.D. Conway, in his *Demonology and Devil-Lore*, asserts that the Scandinavian superstition known as the 'demon-mare' is the source of the use of the horseshoe against witches. In Germany there is a saying in reference to the morbid oppression sometimes experienced during sleep or while dreaming, and which is a symptom of indigestion, 'The nightmare hath ridden thee.'

This elvish mare rides horses also, and in the morning their manes are found all tangled and dripping with sweat.

---

Grimm says that the traditional idea of the Night-mare seems to waver between the ridden animal and the riding, trampling one, precisely as the Devil is sometimes represented as riding men, and again as taking them on his back after the manner of a horse.

---

According to a Bavarian popular belief, the Night-mare is a woman, who is wont to appear at the house door of a morning, invariably requesting the loan of some article. In order to get rid of her at night, one should say: 'Come tomorrow and receive the three white gifts.' The next morning the woman comes, and is given a handful of flour, a handful of salt, and an egg.

In the north of England, naturally perforated stones are hung up by the side of the manger to prevent the Night Hag from riding the horses.

Drink offerings were anciently poured from vessels made from horses' hoofs; and witches are popularly supposed to drink with avidity the water which collects in equine hoof-tracks. German writers on early traditions and folklore agree in ascribing to the horseshoe divers magical properties, whose origin is vaguely connected with the ancient pagan conception of the horse as a sacrificial animal.

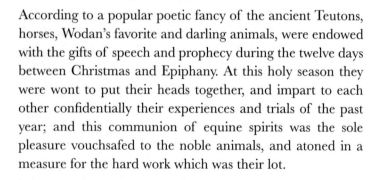

According to a popular poetic fancy of the ancient Teutons, horses, Wodan's favorite and darling animals, were endowed with the gifts of speech and prophecy during the twelve days between Christmas and Epiphany. At this holy season they were wont to put their heads together, and impart to each other confidentially their experiences and trials of the past year; and this communion of equine spirits was the sole pleasure vouchsafed to the noble animals, and atoned in a measure for the hard work which was their lot.

Even nowadays many peasants do not venture to harness their horses at Christmas time, and do not even speak of the animals by name but make use of pet epithets and circumlocutions when they have occasion to refer to them. On Christmas night, hostlers often sleep in the manger or under it, and their dreams at such times are prophetic for the coming year, for in their sleep they can hear what the horses are saying.

———————◆◆◆———————

In order to impart health and vigor to the animals without incurring the expense of extra fodder, the hostler walks at Epiphany season by night three times around the village church, carrying in his uplifted hands a bundle of hay, which he afterwards feeds to the horses; or on Christmas night he steals some cabbage, which is then mixed with the fodder; or, before going to the midnight Christmas Mass, he lays on the manure-heap a quantity of hay called the 'Mass hay', and on his return from church this is given to the horses. Some peasants have a yet more simple method of promoting the welfare of their horses, which consists in laying the cleaning cloth upon a hedge on the evenings of Christmas, New Year's Day, or Epiphany, and afterwards grooming the animals with the dew-laden cloth.

———————◆◆◆———————

In the popular mind horses are credited with extraordinarily keen faculties for detecting ghosts and haunted places, which they instinctively scent from afar. The Thuringian peasant does not beat his horse when the latter refuses to proceed along some gloomy forest road; for the whip is useless against spiritual obstacles, whereas a Paternoster devoutly repeated is usually much more effective.

———————◆◆◆———————

It is a Bohemian superstition that a horse sees everything magnified tenfold, and that this is the reason why the noble animal submits to being led by a little child.

***

When a Brandenburg rustic has bought a horse in a neighboring town and rides him homeward, he dismounts at the boundary line of his own village, and, gathering a handful of his native soil, he throws it backward over the line to prevent the animal's being bewitched. In Bohemia the chief signs of bewitchment in a horse are thought to be shivering, profuse sweating, and emaciation. A charm against this consists in drawing one's shirt inside out over one's head, and using it as a wherewithal to groom the animal – a method which may be acceptable to superstitious jockeys and hostlers, but which will hardly commend itself to a fastidious horse owner.

***

## THE HORSESHOE AS A FAVORITE ANTI-WITCH CHARM

The *universality* of the use of the horseshoe as a safeguard against evil spirits is indeed noteworthy.

It is the anti-witch charm *par excellence*, as well as the approved symbol of good luck, and, used for these purposes, it is to be seen throughout a large portion of the world. The horseshoe is most commonly placed over the entrance doors of dwellings; but stables likewise are thought to be effectually protected by it, for 'witches were dreadful harriers of horseflesh'. In William Henderson's *Folklore of the Northern Countries of England* we read of a Durham farmer who was convinced that one of his horses had been ridden by hags, as he had found it bathed in sweat of a morning. But after he took the precaution to nail a horseshoe over the stable door, and also to hang some broom above the manger, the witches had not been able to indulge in clandestine rides on his horses. While many an honest fellow in England and elsewhere is a firm believer in witches and magical horseshoes, very few of them can give plausible reasons therefore.

———— ⚜ ⚜ ————

The Lancashire farmer thinks that mischievous fairies not only ride horses by night, but drive cows out of the barn, steal the butter, and eat up the children's porridge; so he, too, affixes horseshoes to his buildings.

———— ⚜ ⚜ ————

Anyone visiting the hamlets of Oxfordshire can hardly fail to notice the numerous horseshoes affixed to the picturesque thatched-roofed cottages; and the countryfolk in this neighborhood are not always content with *one* of these popular safeguards, for two or three of them are often to be seen on the walls of a dwelling, invariably placed with the prongs downward.

———— ⚜ ⚜ ————

In John Brand's *Popular Antiquities* may be found a clipping from the Cambridge
*Advertiser*, which relates that one Bartingale, a carpenter and resident of Ely, suspected a woman named Gotobed of having bewitched him, and of being the cause of an illness

which he had recently had. Thereupon, at a consultation of matrons of the neighborhood held in his chamber, it was decided that the most efficient means of protecting him from the evil influence of the suspected sorceress was to have three horseshoes fastened to the door. A blacksmith was accordingly summoned, and an operation to this effect was performed, much to the anger of the supposed witch, who at first complained to the Dean, but was laughed at by his reverence. She then rushed in wrath to the sick man's room, and, miraculous to tell, passed the Rubicon in spite of the horseshoes. But this wonder ceased when it was discovered that Vulcan had substituted donkeys' shoes.

Miss Georgiana F. Jackson says, in *Shropshire Folklore*, that, in the home of her childhood at Edgmond, the stable door was decorated with three rows of horseshoes arranged in the form of a triangle; and the grooms used to say that they were placed there to exclude witches.

In this region, too, an old horseshoe placed above the door of a bedroom is a preventive of the nightmare.

In Shrewsbury, the ancient county town of Shropshire, horseshoe talismans are to be seen not only above the house doors, but also on the barges which navigate the river Severn.

In quite recent times a case has been reported of a poor girl of Whatfield, in Suffolk, who had experienced a long illness, during which she was visited daily by an old woman who appeared to be very solicitous as to her welfare. At length the girl's family began to suspect that this old woman was none other than a witch; they therefore caused a horseshoe to be fastened to the sill of the outer door. The precaution was successful, so runs the tale, for the reputed witch could never thereafter cross the threshold, and the girl speedily recovered her health.

Aubrey, in his *Remains of Gentilisme*, describes the horseshoe as a preservative against the mischief or power of witches, attributing its magical properties to the astrological principle that Mars, the God of War and the War Horse, was an enemy of Saturn, who according to a mediaeval idea was the liege lord of witches.

During the witchcraft excitement in Scotland, one Elizabeth Bathcat was indicted for having a horseshoe attached to the door of her house 'as a devilish means of instruction from the Devil to make her goods and all her other affairs to prosper and succeed well'.

According to an old legend St Dunstan, the versatile English ecclesiastic of the tenth century, who was a skilled farrier and the owner of a forge, was requested by the Devil to shoe his 'single hoof'. Dunstan, who recognized his customer, acceded, but during the operation he caused the Devil so much pain that the latter begged him to desist. The request was heeded on condition that the Devil should never enter a place where a horseshoe was displayed. The popular belief is that his Satanic Majesty has always faithfully kept the contract, and quite naturally all lesser evil spirits have followed his example.

———— ❧ • ❧ ————

In Scotland, even as late as the beginning of the nineteenth century, the peasantry believed that witches were able to draw milk from all the cattle in their neighborhood, by tugging at a hair-rope in imitation of the act of milking. Such a rope was made of hairs from the tails of several cows, whose exact number was indicated by knots in the rope. While tugging at the rope the witches repeated either the following or a similar charm:

> *Cow's milk and mare's milk,*
> *And every beast that bears milk,*
> *Between St Johnstone's and Dundee,*
> *Come a' to me, come a' to me.*

The only adequate protection from such mischievous pranks as these was afforded by nailing a horseshoe to the byre door and tying sprigs of rowan with a red thread to the cow's tail. If, however, these precautions were neglected, the guilty witch might yet be discovered by placing the 'gudeman's breeks' upon the cow's horns, a leg upon either horn; and thereupon the animal, being let loose, was sure to run directly to the witch's house.

———— ❧ • ❧ ————

In many places, certain houses continue even at the present time to have an evil reputation as harborers of witches and goblins. In these cases it seems probable that the owners or occupants of such dwellings neglected to avail themselves of the immunity afforded by horseshoes and other safeguards. For no one, we believe, has ever seriously maintained that evil spirits, who are once firmly domiciled, can be easily expelled. Familiarity with their surroundings may breed a contempt for amulets. Certain it is, however, that an ounce or two of iron by way of prevention is worth a pound or more of cure. When a dwelling is demoniacally possessed, the devils must be driven out somehow, and for this purpose recourse is had to exorcisms, and to religious or magical ceremonies.

In *Antiquitates Vulgares*, by Henry Browne, the writer gives elaborate directions as to the proper mode of exorcising a haunted dwelling, and says that the house which is reported to be vexed with spirits shall be visited by a priest daily for a week, appropriate prayers and scriptural selections being read. Sometimes magical procedures supplanted religious exercises, and experts in sorcery were employed to rid a mansion of its undesirable tenants. The following advertisement from a London newspaper of 1777 may be appropriately given here:

> Haunted Houses – Whereas there are mansions and castles in England and Wales which for many years have been uninhabited, and are now falling into decay, by their being visited and haunted by evil spirits or the spirits of those who for unknown reasons are rendered miserable, even in the grave, a gentleman who has made the tour of Europe, of a particular turn of mind, and deeply skilled in the abstruse and sacred science of exorcism, hereby offers his assistance

to any owner or proprietor of such premises, and undertakes to render the same free from the visitation of such spirits, be their cause what it may, and render them tenantable and useful for the proprietors. Letters addressed to Rev. John Jones, No. 30 St Martin's Lane, duly answered, and interview given if required.

---

It has been supposed that the horseshoe is placed at the outer entrance to a building because of an ancient Saxon superstition that witches were unable successfully to practice their wiles upon persons in the open air. The horseshoe effectively bars the ingress of witches and evil spirits, but an entrance once obtained by these creatures, it is powerless to expel them. Therefore the horseshoe within doors loses much of its efficacy, but is still an emblem of good luck.

---

Edward Moor, in his *Oriental Fragments*, relates having once, in company with a gang of urchins, nailed a donkey-shoe under the threshold of a poor woman in Suffolk who was suspected of sorcery. He and his youthful companions endeavored thus to keep her all night within doors, as witches cannot cross iron.

---

An English writer tells of having heard an animated discussion in the parlor of a London beer-shop as to whether it were preferable to nail a horseshoe behind the door or upon the first doorstep; and instances of extraordinary good luck were mentioned as the direct result of the potency of the amulet in each position.

———————— ⚜ • ⚜ ————————

But there are weighty reasons for the selection of the front door, or the parts immediately connected with it, as the proper place for the display of horseshoes as household guardians.

In the earliest historic times, and in primitive communities, the entrance of a dwelling was considered a sacred place; and in the opinion of eminent scholars who have made a study of the subject, the threshold was the first family altar. A peculiar reverence for the doorway and threshold prevails today in many parts of the world, as is evident from the numerous ceremonial rites in vogue among widely separated savage tribes and uncivilized peoples. Indeed, the custom of placing amulets and charms in and about the entrance doors of houses, stables, and other buildings is almost universal.

———————— ⚜ • ⚜ ————————

In Russia a cross is marked on the threshold to keep witches away.

———————— ⚜ • ⚜ ————————

In Lithuania, when a house is being built, a wooden cross, or some article which has been handed down from past generations, is placed under the threshold. There, also, when a newly baptized child is being brought back from church, it is customary for its father to hold it for a while over the threshold, so as to place the new member of the family under the protection of the domestic divinities. Sick children who are supposed to have been afflicted by an evil eye are washed on the threshold of their cottage, in order that with the help of the *Penates* who reside there, the malady may be driven out of doors.

---

Under the threshold of the Assyrian palaces at Nineveh were found certain images of grotesque monsters, as, for example, a human form with the head of a lynx, and a lion's body with a man's head, which were intended as tutelary deities.

---

In some English counties, naturally perforated stones are hung behind the door; and in Glamorganshire the walls of the houses are whitewashed in order to terrify wandering spirits of evil. Whether successful or not for this purpose, the custom is certainly effective as a destroyer of the demoniac germs of certain diseases.

---

The French Canadians are not the least superstitious of mankind, neither do they wholly neglect to take due precautions against the admittance to their homes of evil spirits. They do not answer '*Entrez*!' when a knock is heard at the door, but call out '*Ouvrez*!' This custom is said to have originated from a current tradition regarding a young woman who once answered '*Entrez*!' in response to a knock, whereupon the Devil promptly came in and carried her away. Where such legends find open-mouthed credence, it does not appear strange that horseshoes and other talismans should be at a premium.

In Tuscany magical medicines are taken upon the threshold, which also plays an important part in sorcery. One reason assigned for this fact is that the threshold forms the line separating the outer world, where demons are rampant, from the domestic precincts, where human beings dwell.

One writer affirms it to be a fixed law in demonology that spirits cannot cross the threshold and enter a house unless previously invited to do so, but adds that there are many exceptions to this rule. The weight of evidence does not support this view, for mischievous fairies and witches are known to rudely disregard the laws of etiquette, and do not wait for an invitation to enter dwellings. This fact is, indeed, a chief *raison d'être* for the use of talismans at the entrance of habitations.

The residents of the beautiful Thuringian Forest region, in whose neighborhood these lines chanced to be penned, are wont to affix horseshoes to the thresholds of their chamber doors, lest some rude goblin enter and disturb their slumbers. But the fastidiousness of these sylvan folk is not content with an ordinary shoe, even though found on the road and venerable with rust; in order to serve its purpose as a talisman, a Thuringian horseshoe must have been forged by a bachelor of wholesome life and good character, on Saint John's Eve.

---

In German households, the horseshoe over the door is believed to afford protection against divers apparitions, as well as against the Devil, witchcraft, lightning, sickness, and evils of every sort.

---

The cross, symbol of the Christian faith, is the most potent of all talismans, but is seldom seen at the entrance of dwellings. In some Roman Catholic countries the crucifix is, indeed, everywhere conspicuous, not only in churches and shrines, but by the roadside, in fields, and on the outer walls of houses, but it is rarely placed at the front door. In Hungary, however, the Magyars mark with black chalk the figure of a cross upon their stable doors, and also brand anew thereon the sacred emblem each year at Christmas time.

---

The respect paid by the inhabitants of Tibet to their household divinities somewhat resembles the worship of their *Lares* by the Romans of old, and finds a parallel in the honor accorded to the favorite amulet of Western civilization, the horseshoe.

The Tibetans set up above the entrances of their houses complex talismans, composed of various mystical objects, such as a ram's skull with horns attached, having displayed

along the base of the skull pieces of carved wood representing
a man and woman, a house, and other symbols; the idea being
to deceive the demons, and to make them believe that these
objects are the real dwelling and its inmates. The Tibetans
believe that the demons are thus tricked, and that the wooden
images are the victims of their mischievous designs.

---

Far away among the nomadic tribes of Turkestan, horseshoes are occasionally seen nailed to the thresholds of
dwellings in the vicinity of the ancient city of Merv; and
within doors, near the entrances of these peculiar habitations, which resemble mammoth parrot cages, pieces of linen
or calico, four or five inches square, are seen upon the felt
wall-lining, to serve as receptacles for the free-will offerings
of such wandering spirits as may pass the magic barriers of
the horseshoes.

---

In some regions there still prevails a time-honored custom
of placing over the chief entrances of dwellings inscriptions, embodying usually a religious thought or exhortation.
Sometimes, however, the sentence commends the house and
its occupants to the care of the goddess Fortune, thus having
a significance akin to that of the horseshoe symbol. In the
year 1892 the writer copied many inscriptions found above
the doors of houses in northern Italy and Switzerland, some
of them being written in Latin, others in German, French,
Italian, and the Romansch dialect, current in the Engadine.
Here, for example, is one from a house in the Swiss village
of Bergun, the original being in German: 'This house is in

God's hand; May Good Luck come in, and Bad Luck stay out! 1673.'

Many of these inscriptions are Biblical verses, which are here used as talismans, just as the pious Muslim employs sentences from the Koran.

Here is the translation of a German sentence over the door of a dwelling in the village of Ober-Schonberg, near Innsbruck, Tyrol, copied in 1897: 'All persons entering this house are recommended to Divine protection. God and the Virgin Mary guard all such, even though powerful enemies threaten, and lightnings and thunder rage without!'

Above the door of a house in the village of Welschnofen, near Botzen, the wayfarer may read the following sentence: 'Pray for us, holy Florian, that fire may not harm our dwelling.' Above the inscription an eye is painted, while below is a realistic picture of Saint Florian, the protector of buildings against fire, engaged in pouring water on a burning roof.

The Bassamese, inhabitants of the Gold Coast of Africa, west of Ashantee, use certain fetish objects for the protection of their dwellings. These amulets, which are often merely pieces of wood painted red, or fragments of pottery, are placed upon the doors of their huts, and are believed to afford ample protection against thieves. Such a fetish is probably intended to exclude evil spirits as well, and is, therefore, a substitute for both the horseshoe and the watch dog, those guardians of the household so popular in civilized communities.

When a modern Egyptian returns from a pilgrimage to Mecca, he fastens above the entrance of his house a branch of the aloe, which is not only a proof of his religious zeal in having accomplished the holy journey, but is also reckoned a protection against objectionable spiritual intruders, and is, therefore, seen in Cairo over the doors of the houses both of Christians and Jews.

In northern Scotland, formerly, a branch of the rowan tree was placed over a farmhouse door, after having been waved while the words 'Avaunt, Satan!' were solemnly pronounced.

About the year 1850 the Rev. Andrew A. Bonar, who was then assistant minister in Collace Parish, Perthshire, Scotland, found the custom of displaying horseshoes on the doors of farm buildings so prevalent that he thought it his duty to remonstrate against a practice savoring of paganism. But his efforts in this direction, though hardly crowned with success, were yet not wholly without avail, for his superstitious parishioners removed the guardian horseshoes from the outsides of the doors, and nailed them up on the insides.

The *raison d'être* of the horseshoe at the entrance of shops and other frequented buildings has been attributed to a belief that, among the many people continually passing through the doorway, someone might, unobserved, bring in ill-luck or work mischief. But these safeguards not only form a sufficient barrier against obnoxious hags and sorcerers, but are potent against ghosts and all manner of evil creatures. When the Oxford undergraduate 'sports his oak' to prevent the untimely entrance of dunning trades people, he shuts out friendly visitors as well; but the faithful horseshoe, by a process of natural selection, debars only objectionable spirits, and is a formidable obstacle to the demon of ill-luck.

---

# THE LUCKY HORSESHOE IN GENERAL

*He laughs like a boor who has found a horseshoe.*
– Dutch proverb

Throughout Germany the belief obtains that a horseshoe found on the road, and nailed on the threshold of a house with the points directed outward, is a mighty protection not only against hags and fiends, but also against fire and lightning; but, reversed, it brings misfortune. In eastern Pennsylvania, however, even in recent times, the horseshoe is often placed with the prongs pointing inward, so that the luck may be spilled into the house. The horseshoe retains its potency as a charm on the sea as well as on land, and it has long been a practice among sailors to nail this favorite amulet against the mast of a vessel, whether fishing-boat or large sea-going craft, as a protection against the Evil One. The shoe of a 'wraith-horse', the mythical offspring of a water-stallion, is especially esteemed by Scotch mariners for this purpose.

In Bohemia only exists the superstition exactly opposite to that elsewhere prevalent, namely, that whoever picks up a horseshoe thereby *ipso facto* picks up ill-luck for himself – a notable example in folklore of the exception which proves the rule. The Bohemians, however, believe a nailed-up horseshoe to be a cure for lunacy.

As a general rule, the degree of luck pertaining to a horseshoe found by chance has been thought to depend on the number of nails remaining in it: the more nails the more luck.

In Northumberland the holes free of nails are carefully counted, as these indicate, presumably in years, how soon the finder of the shoe may expect to be married. The peasants of northern Portugal prefer mule-shoes having an uneven number of nail-holes, as counteractives of the evil influences of the dreaded, omnipresent witches known as the Bruxas.

In Derbyshire it is customary to drive a horseshoe, prongs upward, between two flagstones near the door of a dwelling. This position is sometimes explained by saying that, so placed, the luck cannot spill out.

Farmers may well take heed how they nail up horseshoes over the doors of their barns. To obtain the best results, it would seem advisable to place a pair of these useful articles on each farm building, one with the points upward, the other reversed; for in this way they may not only hope to win Fortune's smiles, but also to keep all witches and unfriendly spirits at a respectful distance.

———◆•◆———

In an interesting story for children in *St Nicholas*, April 1897, by Rudolph F. Bunner, entitled 'The Horseshoe of Luck', the writer introduces Luck in the character and garb of a wandering clown or jester, mounted upon a white horse. This jovial traveler seeks a night's lodging at a wayside farmhouse, and when he has almost reached its hospitable door, his steed casts a shoe, which the farmer hastens to pick up and carefully hangs on a hook above the door. Luck proved to be a most amusing fellow, and after supper he entertained the children of the household in a royal manner, showing them, among other things, how to drop china and glass without breaking them, and how to tumble down stairs without getting hurt. So the evening passed merrily enough, and all retired for the night in a happy frame of mind. Early in the morning the farmer was awakened by the splash of raindrops upon his face, and, hastily arising, he discovered that the roof had sprung a leak, and that his guest had unceremoniously departed. Nettled by such conduct, the farmer and his family hastened in pursuit of the fleeing stranger, guided by the hoofprints of his white horse; and when they had overtaken him, the farmer reproached his late guest for having left his house so abruptly. Whereupon Luck replied: 'I left you, not because you could not even nail my horseshoe over your door, but hung it upside down, so the luck ran out at the ends, but because of your own mistake. You trusted to me; you trusted to Luck. Ah ha!'

In the northernmost districts of Scotland exists a belief that if the first shoe put on the foot of a stallion be hung on the byre door, no harm will come near the cows; and in the same region, if a horseshoe be placed between the houses of quarrelsome neighbors, neither incurs any risk of evil as a result of the other's ill-wishes.

As a means of warding off impending sickness from cattle, and in order that they may thrive during the summer, the Transylvanian peasants place broken horseshoes in the animals' drinking troughs on St John's Day, June 24.

In Lincolnshire, not many years ago, there prevailed a custom of 'charming' ash trees by burying horseshoes under them. Twigs from a tree thus magically endowed were believed to be efficacious in curing cattle over which a shrewmouse had run, or which had been exposed to the glance of an evil eye. To effect a cure in such cases, it was only necessary to gently stroke the affected animal with one of these twigs.

Some years ago, a Golspie fisherman who owned a small boat was favored with an extraordinary run of luck in his fishing, and as a result of his good fortune was enabled to buy a larger vessel, selling the old one to a neighbor. From that time, however, his lucky star seemed to wane, and good 'catches' were infrequent. Casting about in his mind for the reason of this, he bethought him of a stallion's shoe which was fastened inside his former boat, and which had been given him by a 'wise person'. But both boat and horseshoe were now in the hands of his neighbor, who maintained with reason that the lucky token was now his property, as he had purchased 'the boat and its gear'. And ever thereafter the disconsolate fisherman attributed his lack of success in that season to his own folly in having parted with the stallion's shoe.

———— ⚜ ⚜ ————

The horseshoe figures often in traditions of the sea as a protection to sailors. When the ghostly ship of the *Flying Dutchman* meets another vessel, some of its uncanny crew approach the latter in a boat and beg them to take charge of a packet of letters. These letters must be nailed to the mast, else some misfortune will overtake the ship; especially if there be no Bible on board, nor any horseshoe fastened to the foremast.

———— ⚜ ⚜ ————

In the month of September 1825, lightning struck a brigantine which lay at anchor in the Bay of Armiso, in the Adriatic. A sailor was killed by the bolt, and tradition says that on one of his hips was seen the perfect representation of a horseshoe, a counterpart of one nailed to the vessel's foremast in accordance with the custom in vogue on the Mediterranean.

---

The same custom is common in German inland waters, as, for example, on the river craft which ply on the Elbe below Hamburg, and on those which navigate the Trave, at Lubec. On the latter vessels horseshoes are usually fastened to the stern-post, instead of to the mast.

---

In a German work, entitled *Seespuk*, by P.G. Heims, the writer remarks that, among seafaring people, the old pagan emblem, the horseshoe, whose talismanic origin is so closely associated with horse sacrifice and the use of horse flesh as food among the heathen nations of the North, is even now the most powerful safeguard aboard ship against lightning and the powers of evil.

There are comparatively few small vessels laden with wood, fruit, vegetables, or other merchandise, sailing between Baltic Sea ports, upon whose foremast, or elsewhere upon deck, horseshoes are not nailed.

Indeed, continues the same writer, this symbol has a notable significance in German art as well, a fact attributable less to its graceful curving shape than to the deeply rooted superstitions, relics of barbaric times, which yet clung to it.

---

Whether we regard the horseshoe as a symbol of Wodan, the chief deity of the northern nations, as deriving magical power from its half-moon shape, as a product of supernatural skill in dealing with iron and fire, or as appertaining to the favorite sacrificial animal of antiquity, the pagan source of its superstitious use is equally evident.

The horseshoe, whether as an amulet or as a sign of good luck, has nothing to do with the Christian religion. In either case it is a wholly superstitious symbol, and savors of paganism; it is in fact an inheritance from our heathen ancestors, a barbaric token, unworthy even to be named in connection with the sacred cross. Yet throughout many centuries it has captivated the popular fancy, and its emblematic use appears to be as firmly established today as ever in many parts of the world.

---

It is popularly believed that the chance finding of a horseshoe greatly enhances its magical power; and it is claimed, moreover, by some writers, to be an axiom in folklore that talismanic objects thrust upon one's notice, as it were, are direct gifts from the goddess Fortune, and hence possessed of a special value for the finder. Such a notion is as clearly of pagan origin as the custom of bowing to the new moon, or of fixing representations of horses' heads upon the gables of houses in order to terrify wandering spirits of evil.

---

In *Curiosities of Popular Customs*, by William S. Walsh, it is stated that the Northern peoples were wont to offer sacrifices to Wodan after the harvest, and that the little cakes still baked on St Martin's Day, November 11, throughout Germany, are shaped like a horn or horseshoe, which was a token of the pagan god. Although not susceptible of proof, it seems highly probable that we have here another relic of idolatry. It is a point worthy of note, moreover, that Wodan was not only an all-powerful deity, corresponding to the Greek Zeus and Roman Jupiter, but that he was also a great magician, and hence quite naturally the horseshoe, as one of his symbols, inherits magical attributes.

---

In Tuscany a horseshoe when found is placed in a small red bag with some hay, which the Tuscans consider also a luck-bringing article, and the twofold charm is kept in its owner's bed.

---

Dr Robert James, an English physician of the eighteenth century, and the inventor of a well-known fever powder, ascribed his success in acquiring a fortune to his good luck in having once found a horseshoe on Westminster Bridge. The sincerity of his faith was attested by the adoption of the horseshoe as his family crest.

---

In some Roman Catholic countries the priests are wont to brand cows and pigs on the forehead with the mark of a horseshoe, to insure them against disease. It was, moreover, an old Scotch superstition, or *freet*, to pass a horseshoe thrice beneath the belly and over the back of a cow that was considered elf-shot.

---

Among the Wendish inhabitants of the Spreewald, in North Germany, the lucky finder of a horseshoe is careful not to tell any neighbor of his good fortune, but proceeds at once to fasten the shoe over the door of his house, or on the threshold, with three nails, and by three blows of a hammer, so that evil spirits may not enter.

We have seen that a horseshoe picked up on the road is often prized as no mean acquisition by the finder thereof. It may not be out of place to give here a literal translation of a spell for the protection of a horse's hoof when a shoe has been lost. The original appeared in Mone's *Anzeiger* in 1834, and is written in the dialect known as 'Middle High German', which was in vogue from the twelfth to the sixteenth centuries:

> When a horse has lost one of its iron shoes, take a breadknife and incise the hoof at the edge from one heel to the other, and lay the knife crosswise on the sole and say: 'I command thee, hoof and horn, that thou breakest as little as God the Lord broke his Word, when he created heaven and earth.' And thou shalt say these words three hours in succession, and five Paternosters and five Ave Marias to the praise of the Virgin. Then the horse will not walk lame until thou happenest to reach a smithy.

The Germans have a saying in regard to a young girl who has been led astray, 'She has lost a horseshoe.' This saying has been associated with the shoe as a symbol of marriage, an idea found both in the northern and Indian mythologies. But the phrase has been also thought to refer to the horseshoe shaped *gloria* which crowns the head of the Virgin, the horseshoe thus becoming the symbol of maidenly chastity. Again, it has been suggested, in reference to the same phrase, that the horseshoe is a symbol of the V (or first letter of the word Virgo), which is used in church records to designate the unmarried state, just as the word 'spinster' is used in legal documents.

The ancient Irish were wont to hang up in their houses the feet and legs of their deceased steeds, setting an especial value upon the hoofs; and with the Chinese of today a horse's hoof hung up indoors is supposed to have the same protective influence over a dwelling that a horseshoe has elsewhere. In south-western Germany it is still a common practice to nail a hoof over the stable door; and in the Netherlands a horse's foot placed in a stable is thought to keep the horses from being bewitched.

Burton, in his *Anatomy of Melancholy*, admits a belief in the virtues of a ring made from the hoof of the right foot of an ass, when carried about as an amulet.

Occasionally, though rarely, the horseshoe is thought to have been employed by the witches themselves in furtherance of their mischievous designs.

———— ❖ · ❖ ————

In the *Revue des traditions populaires*, an anecdote is related of a veteran Polish cavalry-man who had served under Napoleon I. While bivouacking with a detachment of lancers in a village of eastern Prussia, he and several others lodged in the house of an old peasant woman, and their horses were accommodated in her barn. It was shortly noticed that the animals appeared depressed and refused the hay and grain provided for them, whereupon the soldiers concluded that they were under some spell and began a search for the cause. They soon found an old horseshoe with three nails remaining in it, and one of these was quickly driven out with a hammer. Instantly the horses began to snort and exhibited signs of restlessness. On the removal of the second nail they held up their heads proudly, and when the third nail was hammered out they fell upon their provender and devoured it voraciously. The cavalrymen were now convinced that their horses had been the victims of some deviltry at the hands of their hostess, whom they believed to be a sorceress. Before their departure, therefore, they gave her a good beating with their sabre scabbards to teach her not to practice her nefarious arts upon the horses of honest people.

———— ❖ · ❖ ————

## CONCLUSION

Whatever may be the origin of the superstitious employment of the horseshoe, its adoption as a token of good luck appears to be comparatively modern, its earliest use having been for the exclusion of witches, evil spirits, and all such uncanny beings.

Before leaving the subject an extract may be given from an article in the *London World*, August 23, 1753, against the repeal of the so-called Witch Act, wherein the writer offers the following satirical advice to whomever it might concern:

> To secure yourself against the enchantments of witches, especially if you are a person of fashion and have never been taught the Lord's Prayer, the only method I know of is to nail a horseshoe upon the threshold. This I can affirm to be of the greatest efficacy, insomuch that I have taken notice of many a little cottage in the country with a horseshoe at its door where gaming, extravagance, Jacobitism, and all the catalogue of witchcrafts have been totally unknown.

The world moves and civilization progresses, but the old superstitions remain the same. The rusty horseshoe found on the road is still prized as a lucky token, and will doubtless continue to be so prized; for human nature does not change, and superstition is a part of human nature.

# FORTUNE AND LUCK

*Since Fortune is not in our power,*
*Let us be as little as possible in hers.*
– Steele.

## LUCK, ANCIENT AND MODERN

Our English word luck, according to some authorities, is of Scandinavian origin, while others consider it to be the past tense of an Anglo-Saxon verb meaning 'to catch'. Luck signifies, therefore, a good catch, and is analogous to the German *Glück*. It has been aptly remarked that very many so-called strong-minded persons, who would not for a moment admit that they are superstitious, are yet not insensible to the fascination of this little monosyllable. As Christian people, we profess to believe implicitly in Divine Providence; yet often because we cannot understand its workings, we so far relapse into paganism as to worship secretly the Goddess Fortune. The fact is, that superstition is an ineradicable element of human nature. The combined forces of religion, education, philosophy, and common sense are allied in a perpetual warfare against it. The thousand and one little credulities which form such an important part of modern folklore may be intrinsically the veriest whimsies and trifles, but they are evidence of the tenacity of traditional beliefs.

The modern sailor carries in his pocket a bit of seal-skin, or an eagle's beak, to shield him from the lightning; and the Southern negro has his rabbit's foot, and a host of other outlandish fetishes, all for luck.

---

The millions of American negroes have, indeed, a deeply-rooted love for the supernatural, and their character exhibits a peculiar blending of superstition and religion. Among the mixed colored races in Missouri, for example, we find a bewildering jumble of African Voodoo credulities, the traditions of the American Indian, and religious fanaticism. Thus, in *Voodoo Tales*, by Mary A. Owen, we read of an old crone who kept her medicine pipe and eagle-bone whistle alongside of her books of devotion, carried a rosary and rabbit's foot in the same pocket, and wore a saint's toe dangling on her bosom, and a luck-ball under her right arm.

---

It has been well said that only those whose minds are predisposed to entertain idle fancies are wont to regard misfortune as a natural sequence of the legion of alleged evil omens. Yet we know that in all ages and countries such notions have prevailed. The ancient Chaldeans made use of magic formulae to ward off ill-luck, and Tacitus relates that the most trivial events were regarded as portentous by the Roman people. What a contrast to the credulity of a superstitious age is afforded by the often quoted remark of Cato the Censor, who refused to regard it as ominous when informed that his boots had been gnawed by rats! 'If the boots had gnawed the rats,' he said, 'it might have portended evil.'

---

There is a deal of philosophy in the Irish saying, 'Every man has bad luck awaiting him some time or other, but leave the bad luck to the last; perhaps it may never come.'

---

In attributing the sundry and divers misfortunes of our lives to bad luck, we surely ignore the fact that these same unwelcome experiences are often the logical sequences of our own shortcomings, and that the fickle goddess cannot with fairness be made always to masquerade as our scapegoat.

---

# THE FOLKLORE OF COMMON SALT

*Jests, like salt, should be used sparingly.*
– Similitudes of Democritus.

## ORIGIN AND HISTORY

The origin of the use of common salt as a condiment is hidden in the mazes of antiquity. Although we have no evidence that this important article of diet was known to the antediluvians, there is still abundant proof that it was highly esteemed as a seasoner of food long before the Christian era. In a Greek translation of a curious fragment of the writings of the semi-fabulous Phoenician author, Sanchoniathon, who is said to have lived before the Trojan War, the discovery of the uses of salt is attributed to certain immediate descendants of Noah, one of whom was his son Shem.

---

From the mythical lore of Finland we learn that Ukko, the mighty god of the sky, struck fire in the heavens, a spark from which descending was received by the waves and became salt. The Chinese worship an Idol called Phelo, in honor of a mythological personage of that name, whom they believe to have been the discoverer of salt and the originator of its use. His ungrateful countrymen, however, were tardy in their recognition of Phelo's merits, and that worthy thereupon left his native land and did not return. Then the Chinese declared him to be a deity, and in the month of June each year they hold a festival in his honor, during which he is everywhere eagerly sought, but in vain; he will not appear until he comes to announce the end of the world.

———— ❖••❖ ————

Among the Mexican Nahuas the women and girls employed in the preparation of salt were wont to dance at a yearly festival held in honor of the Goddess of salt, Huixtocihuatl, whose brothers the rain-gods are said, as the result of a quarrel, to have driven her into the sea, where she invented the art of making the precious substance.

———— ❖••❖ ————

The earliest Biblical mention of salt appears to be in reference to the destruction of Sodom and Gomorrah. When King Abimelech destroyed the city of Shechem, an event which is believed to have occurred in the thirteenth century BC, he is said to have 'sowed salt on it', this phrase expressing the completeness of its ruin. It is certain that the use of salt as a relish was known to the Jewish people at a comparatively early period of their history. For in the sixth chapter of the Book of Job occurs this passage: 'Can that which is unsavoury be eaten without salt?'

———— ❖••❖ ————

In Eastern countries it is a time-honored custom to place salt before strangers as a token and pledge of friendship and good-will. The phrase 'to eat someone's salt' formerly signified being in that person's service, and in this sense it is used in the Book of Ezra, iv. 14, where the expression, 'we have maintenance from the king's palace', means literally, 'we are salted with the salt of the palace', which implies being in the service of the king. And from the idea of being in the employment of a master, and eating his salt, the phrase in question came to denote faithfulness and loyalty.

---

As an instance of the superstitious reverence with which salt is regarded in the East, it is related that Yacoub ben Laith, who founded the dynasty of Persian princes known as the Saffarides, was of very humble origin, and in his youth gained a livelihood as a free-booter. Yet so chivalrous was he that he never stripped his victims of all their belongings, but always left them something to begin life with anew.

On one occasion this gallant robber had forcibly and by stealth entered the palace of a prince, and was about departing with considerable spoil, when he stumbled over an object which his sense of taste revealed to be a lump of salt. Having thus involuntarily partaken of a pledge of hospitality in another man's house, his honor overcame his greed of gain and he departed without his booty.

---

Owing to its antiseptic and preservative qualities, salt was emblematic of durability and permanence; hence the expression 'Covenant of Salt'. It was also a symbol of wisdom, and in this sense was doubtless used by St Paul when he told the Colossians that their speech should be seasoned with salt.

Homer called salt divine, and Plato described it as a substance dear to the gods.

Perhaps the belief in its divine attributes may have been a reason for the employment of salt as a sacrificial offering by the Hebrews, Greeks, and Romans, all of whom, moreover, regarded it as an indispensable relish.

Plutarch said that without salt nothing was savory or toothsome, and that this substance even imparted an additional flavor to wines, thus causing them 'to go down the throat merrily'. And the same writer remarked that, as bread and salt were commonly eaten together, therefore Ceres and Neptune were sometimes worshiped together in the same temple.

## SALT UNCONGENIAL TO WITCHES AND DEVILS

Grimm remarks that salt is not found in witches' kitchens, nor at devils' feasts, because the Roman Catholic Church has taken upon herself the hallowing and dedication of this substance. Moreover, inasmuch as Christians recognize salt as a wholesome and essential article of diet, it seems plausible enough that they should regard it as unsuitable for the use of devils and witches, two classes of beings with whom they have no particular sympathy. Hence perhaps the familiar saying that 'the Devil loveth no salt in his meat'.

---

Once upon a time, according to tradition, there lived a German peasant whose wife was a witch, and the Devil invited them both to supper one fine evening. All the dishes lacked seasoning, and the peasant, in spite of his wife's remonstrances, kept asking for salt; and when after a while it was brought, he remarked with fervor, 'Thank God, here is salt at last,' whereupon the whole scene vanished.

---

The abbot Richalmus, who lived in the old German duchy of Franconia in the twelfth century, claimed, by the exercise of a special and extraordinary faculty, to be able to baffle the machinations of certain evil spirits who took special delight in playing impish tricks upon churchmen. They appear, indeed, to have sorely tried the patience of the good abbot in many ways, as, for example, by distracting his thoughts during Mass and interfering with his digestion, promoting discords in the church music, and causing annoyance by inciting the congregation to cough in sermon time. Fortunately he possessed three efficient weapons against these troublesome creatures, namely, the sign of the cross, holy water, and salt.

'Evil spirits,' wrote the abbot, 'cannot bear salt.' When he was at dinner, and the Devil had maliciously taken away his appetite, he simply tasted a little salt, and at once became hungry. Then, if soon afterwards his appetite again failed him, he took some more salt, and his relish for food speedily returned.

---

In Hungarian folklore, contrary to the usual opinion, evil personages are fond of salt, for at those festive gatherings described in old legends and fairy tales, where witches and the Devil met, they were wont to cook in large kettles a stew of horse-flesh seasoned with salt, upon which they eagerly feasted.

Hence appears to have originated the popular notion current among the Magyars that a woman who experiences a craving for salt in the early morning must be a witch, and on no account should her taste be gratified.

———— ✦ · ✦ ————

Once upon a time, says tradition, a man crept into a witch's tub in order to spy upon the proceedings at a meeting of the uncanny sisterhood. Shortly thereafter the witch appeared, saddled the tub, and rode it to the place of rendezvous, and on arriving there the man contrived to empty a quantity of salt into the tub. After the revels he was conveyed homewards in the same manner, and showed the salt to his neighbors as proof positive that he had really been present at the meeting. Sometimes, however, salt is used in Hungary as a protection against witches. The threshold of a new house is sprinkled with it, and the door- hinges are smeared with garlic, so that no witch may enter.

———— ✦ · ✦ ————

The peasants of Russian Estonia are aware of the potency of salt against witches and their craft. They believe that on St John's Eve witch-butter is maliciously smeared on the doors of their farm buildings in order to spread sickness among the cattle. When, therefore, an Estonian farmer finds this obnoxious butter on his barn door or elsewhere, he loads his gun with salt and shoots the witch germs away.

———— ✦ ————

The Hindus have a theory that malignant spirits, or Bhuts, are especially prone to molest women and children immediately after the latter have eaten confectionery and other sweet delicacies.

Indeed, so general is this belief that vendors of sweetmeats among school children provide their youthful customers each with a pinch of salt to remove the sweet taste from their mouths, and thus afford a safeguard against the ever-watchful Bhuts.

———— ✦ ————

## THE LATIN WORD 'SAL'

Owing to the importance of salt as a relish, its Latin name *sal* came to be used metaphorically as signifying a savory mental morsel, and, in a general sense, wit or sarcasm. It was formerly maintained by some etymologists that this word had a threefold meaning according to its gender. Thus, when masculine, it has the above signification, but when feminine it means the sea, and only when neuter does it stand for common salt. The characterization of Greece as 'the salt of nations' is attributed to Livy, and this is probably the origin of the phrase 'Attic salt', meaning delicate, refined wit. The phrase *cum grano salis* may signify the grain of common sense with which one should receive a seemingly exaggerated report. It may also mean moderation, even as salt is used sparingly as a seasoner of food.

---

Among the ancients, as with ourselves, *sol* and *sal*, the sun and salt, were known to be two things essential to the maintenance of life. Soldiers, officials, and working people were paid either wholly or in part in salt, which was in such general use for this purpose that any sum of money paid for labor or service of whatever kind was termed a *solarium*, or salary, that is, the wherewithal to obtain one's salt.

Pliny remarked that salt was essential for the complete enjoyment of life, and in confirmation of this statement he commented on the fact that the word sales was employed to express the pleasures of the mind, or a keen appreciation of witty effusions, and, therefore, was associated with the idea of good fellowship and mirth.

---

A certain mystic significance has been attributed to the three letters composing the word 'sal'. Thus, the letter S, standing alone, represents or suggests two circles united together, the sun and the moon. It typifies, moreover, the union of things divine and mundane, even as salt partakes of the attributes of each. A, alpha, signifies the beginning of all things; while L is emblematic of something celestial and glorious. S and L represent solar and lunar influences respectively, and the trio of letters stand for an essential substance provided by God for the benefit of his people. In a curious treatise on salt, originally published in 1770, the writer launches forth in impassioned style the most extravagant encomiums upon this substance, which he avers to be the quintessence of the earth. Salt is here characterized as a Treasure of

Nature, an Essence of Perfection, and the Paragon of Preservatives. Moreover, whoever possesses salt thereby secures a prime factor of human happiness among material things.

———— ❧ ❧ ————

The French people employ the word 'salt' metaphorically in several common expressions. Thus, in speaking of the lack of piquancy or pointedness in a dull sermon or address, they say, 'There was no salt in that discourse.' And of the brilliant productions of a favorite author they remark, 'He has sprinkled his writings with salt by handfuls.' In like manner they use the term *un epigramme salé* to denote a cutting sarcasm or raillery. Very apt also is the following definition by an old English writer: 'Salt, a pleasaunt and merrie word that maketh folks to laugh and sometime pricketh.' The expression 'to salt an invoice' signifies to increase the full market value of each article, and corresponds to one use of the French verb *saler*, to overcharge, and hence to 'fleece' or 'pluck'. Thus the phrase '*Il me la bien salé*' means 'He has charged me an excessive price.'

———— ❧ ❧ ————

## SALT EMPLOYED TO CONFIRM AN OATH

In the records of the Presbytery of Edinburgh, under date of September 20, 1586, is to be found the following description of an oath which Scotch merchants were required to take when on their way to the Baltic:

> Certan merchantis passing to Danskerne
> (Denmark) and cuming neir Elsinnure, chusing
> out and quhen they accompted for the payment
> of the toill of the goods, and that depositioun of
> ane othe in forme following, viz: Thei present
> and offer breid and salt to the deponer of the
> othe, whereon he layis his hand and deponis his
> conscience and sweiris.

---

Gypsies likewise sometimes use bread and salt to confirm the solemnity of an oath. An example of this is recorded in the 'Pesther Lloyd' of July 1, 1881. A member of a gypsy band in western Hungary had been robbed of a sum of money, and so informed his chief, who summoned the elders of the camp to a council. On an upright cross formed of two poles was placed a piece of bread sprinkled with salt, and upon this each gypsy was required to swear that he was not the thief. The real culprit, refusing to take so solemn an oath, was thus discovered.

---

Among the Jews the covenant of salt is the most sacred possible. Even at the present time, Arabian princes are wont to signify their ratification of an alliance by sprinkling salt upon bread, meanwhile exclaiming, 'I am the friend of thy friends, and the enemy of thine enemies.' So likewise there is a common form of request among the Arabs as follows: 'For the sake of the bread and salt which are between us, do this or that.'

---

In the East, at the present day, compacts between tribes are still confirmed by salt, and the most solemn pledges are ratified by this substance. During the Indian mutiny of 1857 a chief motive of self-restraint among the Sepoys was the fact that they had sworn by their salt to be loyal to the English queen.

---

The antiquity of the practice of using salt in confirmation of an oath is shown in the following passage from an ode of the Greek lyric poet Archilochus, who flourished during the early part of the seventh century BC: 'Thou hast broken the solemn oath, and hast disgraced the salt and the table.'

---

In the year 1731 the Protestant miners and peasants inhabiting the 'salt exchequer lands', prior to their banishment from the country by Leopold, Archbishop of Salzburg, held a meeting in the picturesque village of Schwarzach, and 'solemnly ratified their league by the ancient custom of dipping their fingers in salt.' The table at which this ceremony took place, and a picture representing the event, are still shown at the Wallner Inn, where the meeting was held.

---

## SALT-SPILLING AS AN OMEN

The widespread notion that the spilling of salt produces evil consequences is supposed to have originated in the tradition that Judas overturned a salt cellar at the Paschal Supper, as portrayed in Leonardo da Vinci's painting. But it appears more probable that the belief is due to the sacred character of salt in early times. Anyone having the misfortune to spill salt was formerly supposed to incur the anger of all good spirits, and to be rendered susceptible to the malevolent influences of demons. When, in oriental lands, salt was offered to guests as a token of hospitality, it was accounted a misfortune if any particles were scattered while being so presented, and in such cases a quarrel or dispute was anticipated.

———— ❧ ❧ ————

Bishop Hall wrote, in 1627, that when salt fell towards a superstitious guest at dinner, he was wont to exhibit signs of mental agitation, and refused to be comforted until one of the waiters had poured wine in his lap. And in Gayton's 'Art of Longevity' we find these lines: 'I have two friends of either sex, which do eat little salt or none, yet are friends too; of both which persons I can truly tell, they are of patience most invincible; whom out of temper no mischance at all can put; no, if towards them the salt should fall.'

———— ❧ ❧ ————

The Germans have a saying, 'Whoever spills salt arouses enmity,' and in some places the overthrow of a salt cellar is thought to be the direct act of the Devil, the peace-disturber. The superstitious Parisian, who may have been the unfortunate cause of such a mishap, is quite ready to adopt this view, and tosses a little of the spilled salt behind him, in order, if possible, to hit the invisible Devil in the eye, which, temporarily at least, prevents him from doing further mischief. This is probably a relic of an ancient idolatrous custom; and salt thus thrown was formerly a kind of sop to

Cerberus, an offering to pacify some particular deity. In like manner the natives of Pegu, a province of British Burmah, in the performance of one of their rites in honor of the Devil, are wont to throw food over their left shoulders to conciliate the chief spirit of evil.

---

When salt was spilled at table the pious Roman was wont to exclaim, 'May the gods avert the omen!' and the modern Sicilian, in such a case, invokes 'the Mother of Light'.

---

Among the Greeks it was customary to present salt to the gods as a thank-offering at the beginning of every meal. Louis Figuier, in 'Les merveilles de l'industrie', places these three happenings in the category of ominous mishaps in a Grecian household: (1) the omission of a salt cellar from among the furnishings of a dinner table; (2) the falling asleep of one of the guests at a banquet, before the removal of the salt cellar to make place for the dessert; (3) the overturning of this important vessel. It seems evident, therefore, that the origin of the belief in the ominous character of salt spilling is of far greater antiquity than is popularly supposed; and Leonardo da Vinci, in portraying Judas as upsetting a salt cellar, probably had in mind the already well-known portentous significance of such an act. But some observers have failed to discover any trace of a salt-cellar in the original Cenacolo on the refectory wall of the Milanese convent. In the well-known engraving by Raphael Morghen, however, the overthrown salt cellar is clearly delineated, and the spilled salt is seen issuing from it.

———— ❧ • ❧ ————

In Gaule's *Magastromancer* overturning the salt is mentioned in a list of 'superstitious ominations'. According to a popular Norwegian belief, one will shed as many tears as may suffice to dissolve the quantity of salt which he has spilled; and in east Yorkshire, also, every grain of spilled salt represents a tear to be shed. Moreover, saltness has been thought to be an essential attribute of tears, and this intimate connection between the two may have given rise to some of the many superstitions connected with salt.

———— ❧ • ❧ ————

In Bucks County, Pennsylvania, in order to avert ill-luck after salt has been spilled, one should not only toss a pinch of the spilled salt over the left shoulder, but should also crawl under a table and come out on the opposite side.

———— ❧ • ❧ ————

In New England the gravity of salt-spilling as an omen, its deplorable severance of friendship's ties, and the necessity for prompt remedial measures, are all fully recognized.

And here the deft toss of the spilled particles over the left shoulder is not always adequate; for in order thoroughly to break the spell, these particles must be thrown on the stove.

———— ❧ • ❧ ————

Gypsies have a saying, 'The salt of strife has fallen.' From the idea of the desecration of a sacred substance, to which allusion has been made, doubtless arose the remarkable superstition that, as a penalty for spilling salt, one must wait outside the gate of Paradise for as many years as there are grains of salt spilled.

***

# HELPING TO
# SALT AT TABLE

In the northern counties of England, and indeed quite generally in Anglican communities, it is reckoned unlucky to be helped to salt at table, and this idea has found expression in the popular couplet, 'Help me to salt, help me to sorrow.' In a small volume entitled *The Rules of Civility* translated from the French, and quoted in *Brand's Popular Antiquities*, is the following passage:

> Some are so exact they think it uncivil to help anybody that sits by them either with *salt* or *brains*. But in my judgment that is a ridiculous scruple, and if your neighbor desires you to furnish him with salt you must either take out some with your knife and lay it upon his plate, or if they be more than one, present them with the salt that they may furnish themselves.

***

In Russia there is a superstitious prejudice against helping one's neighbor to salt at table on account of the liability to quarrels thereby incurred. For in so doing one is thought to have the air of implying, 'Well, you have received your allowance of salt, now go away.' But if in proffering the salt one smiles amicably, all danger of a quarrel is happily averted, and the act is wholly relieved of its ominous character.

The simple expedient of a second help is commonly regarded as equally effective for this purpose, but it is difficult to imagine whence was derived the alleged potency of such an antidote, which is contrary to the Pythagorean theory of the divine character of unity and the diabolical attributes of the number two.

In many lands, however, it is only common courtesy to help a friend to salt at table; but in Italy this delicate attention was formerly thought to be a mark of undue familiarity, and, when salt was offered by one gentleman to the wife of another, it was a sufficient cause for jealousy and even quarrel.

## SALT AS A PROTECTION
## TO YOUNG INFANTS

The mediaeval Roman Catholic custom of using salt to protect infants from evil prior to their baptism is frequently alluded to in early romantic literature. In an ancient ballad entitled 'The King's Daughter', the birth of a child occurs under circumstances which prevent the administration of the rite of baptism. The mother, therefore, exposes the baby in a casket, and is careful to place by its side salt and candles. The words of the ballad are:

> *The bairnie she swyl'd in linen so fine,*
> *In a gilded casket she laid it syne,*
> *Mickle saut and light she laid therein.*
> *Cause yet in God's house it had'na been.*

---

Mr William G. Black, in his work on folk medicine, says that in some districts of Scotland it was formerly a custom, previous to baptism, to carry some salt around the child 'withershins', or backwards, a procedure which was believed to protect the child from evil during its oftentimes long journey from the house to the church where the ceremony was to be performed.

---

In Marsala the relatives of a newborn child do not sleep the first night, for fear of the appearance of witches. Indeed, a watch is often kept for many nights, or until the child's baptism. A light burns in the room constantly, and an image of some saint is fastened upon the house door. A rosary and a raveled napkin are attached to the image, and behind the door are placed a jug of salt and a broom. When a witch comes and sees the saint's image and the rosary, she usually goes away at once; but even if these talismans are wanting, the salt, napkin, and broom afford adequate protection. For any witch before entering must count the grains of salt, the threads of the napkin's fringe, and the twigs of which the broom is made. And she never has time enough for these tasks, because she cannot appear before midnight, and must hide herself before the dawn.

---

This popular belief in the magical power of salt to protect infants from evil, especially in the period between birth and baptism, is exemplified in the following allusion to a foundling in a metrical *History of the Family of Stanley*, which dates from the early part of the sixteenth century: 'It was uncrisned, seeming out of doubt, for salt was bound at its neck in a linen clout.'

---

In Sicily, too, it is sometimes customary for the priest to place a little salt in the child's mouth at baptism, thereby imparting wisdom. Hence the popular local saying in regard to a person who is dull of understanding, that the priest put but little salt in his mouth.

---

A similar usage is in vogue in the district of Campine in Belgium. The use of salt at baptism in the Christian Church dates from the fourth century. It was an early practice to place salt, which had been previously blessed, in the infant's mouth, to symbolize the counteraction of the sinfulness of its nature.

---

So, too, in the baptismal ceremonies of the Church of England in mediaeval times, salt, over which an exorcism had been said, was placed in the child's mouth, and its ears and nostrils were touched with saliva, practices which became obsolete at about the time of the reign of Henry VIII.

An octagonal font of the fifteenth century, in St Margaret's Church, Ipswich, Suffolk, has upon one of its sides the figure of an angel bearing a scroll, on which appears a partially illegible inscription containing the words *Sal et Saliva*.

---

Thomas Ady, in 'A Perfect Discovery of Witches', says that holy water, properly conjured, was used to keep the Devil in awe, and to prevent his entering churches or dwellings.

With such holy water Satanic influences were kept away from meat and drink, and from 'the very salt upon the table'.

---

In the Highlands of Scotland, instead of using salt as an amulet for the protection of young babies, it was customary for watchers to remain constantly by the cradle until the christening. For it was believed that spiteful fairies were wont to carry off healthy infants, leaving in their stead puny specimens of their own elfish offspring; and infants thus kidnapped were sometimes kept in fairyland for seven years. This well-known popular belief gave rise to the word 'changeling', which signifies a 'strange, stupid, ugly child left by the fairies in place of a beautiful or charming child that they have stolen away'.

---

# SALT AS A
# MAGICAL SUBSTANCE

The natives of Morocco regard salt as a talisman against evil, and a common amulet among the Neapolitan poor is a bit of rock salt suspended from the neck.

The peasants of the Hartz Mountain region in Germany believe that three grains of salt in a milk-pot will keep witches away from the milk; and to preserve butter from their uncanny influences, it was a custom in the county of Aberdeen, Scotland, some years ago, to put salt on the lid of a churn.

In Normandy, also, the peasants are wont to throw a little salt into a vessel containing milk, in order to protect the cow who gave the milk from the influences of witchcraft.

Peculiar notions about the magical properties of salt are common among American negroes. Thus in some regions a new tenant will not move into a furnished house until all objects therein have been thoroughly salted, with a view to the destruction of witch germs.

Another example of the supernatural attributes ascribed to salt is the opinion current among uneducated people in some communities of its potency in casting a spell over obnoxious individuals. For this purpose it is sufficient either to sprinkle salt over the sleeping form of an enemy, or on the grave of one of his ancestors. Another kind of salt spell in vogue in the south of England consists in throwing a little salt into the fire on three successive Friday nights, while saying these words:

> *It is not this salt I wish to burn,*
> *It is my lover's heart to turn;*
> *That he may neither rest nor happy be,*
> *Until he comes and speaks to me.*

On the third Friday night the disconsolate damsel expects her lover to appear. Everyone is familiar with the old saying, 'You can catch a bird with your hand, if you first put some salt on its tail.' This quaint expression has been thought to imply that, if one can get near enough to a bird to place salt on its tail, its capture is an easy matter. The phrase, however, may be more properly attributed to a belief in the magical properties of salt in casting a spell over the bird. Otherwise any substance might be equally effective for the purpose of catching it. The writer remembers having read somewhere an old legend about a young man who playfully threw some salt on the back of a witch sitting next to him at table, and the witch thereupon acquired such an increase of avoirdupois that she was unable to move until the young man obligingly brushed away the salt.

---

The ancient Teutons believed that the swift flight of birds was caused by certain powerful spirits of the air. Now salt is a foe to ghostly might, imparts weight to bodies, and impedes their motion; therefore the rationale of its operation when placed upon a bird's tail is easily intelligible.

———— ❧ • ❧ ————

In the Province of Quebec French Canadians sometimes scatter salt about the doors of their stables to prevent those mischievous little imps called *lutins* from entering and teasing the horses by sticking burrs in their manes and tails. The *lutin* or *gobelin* is akin to the Scandinavian household spirit, who is fond of children and horses, and who whips and pinches the former when they are naughty, but caresses them when good.

———— ❧ • ❧ ————

In Marsala, west Sicily, a horse, mule, or donkey, on entering a new stall, is thought to be liable to molestation by fairies. As a precautionary measure, therefore, a little salt is placed on the animal's back, and this is believed to insure freedom from lameness, or other evil resulting from fairy spite.

———— ❧ • ❧ ————

Common salt has long enjoyed a reputation as a means of procuring disenchantment. It was an ingredient of a salve 'against nocturnal goblin visitors' used by the Saxons in England, and described in one of their ancient leech books; while in the annals of folk medicine are to be found numerous references to its reputed virtues as a magical therapeutic agent.

———— ❧ • ❧ ————

In Scotland, when a person is ailing of some affection whose nature is not apparent, as much salt as can be placed on a sixpence is dissolved in water, and the solution is then applied three times to the soles of the patient's feet, to the palms of his hands, and to his forehead. He is then expected to taste the mixture, a portion of which is thrown over the fire while saying, 'Lord, preserve us frae a' skaith.'

---

The Germans of Buffalo valley in central Pennsylvania believe that a boy may be cured of homesickness by placing salt in the hems of his trousers and making him look up the chimney.

---

In India the natives rub salt and wine on the affected part of the body as a cure for scorpion bites, believing that the success of this treatment is due to the supernatural virtue of the salt in scaring away the fiends who caused the pain. An ancient Irish charm of great repute in cases of suspected 'fairy stroke' consisted in placing on a table three equal portions of salt in three parallel rows. The would-be magician then encircles the salt with his arm and repeats the Lord's Prayer thrice over each row. Then, taking the hand of the fairy-struck person, he says over it, 'By the power of the Father and of the Son and of the Holy Spirit, let this disease depart and the spell of evil spirits be broken.' Then follows a solemn adjuration and command addressed to the supposed demon, and the charm is complete.

---

In Bavaria and the Ukraine, in order to ascertain whether a child has been the victim of bewitchment, the mother licks its forehead; and if her sense of taste reveals thereby a marked saline flavor, she is convinced that her child has been under the influence of an evil eye.

In the Swiss canton of Bern a person is believed to be amply fortified against all kinds of spiritual enemies by the simple expedient of carrying a piece of fresh bread and a psalm book in the right and left coat pockets respectively, provided one is careful to have some rock-salt either in each vest pocket, or inside a briar-wood cane upon which three crosses have been cut. In Bohemia a mother seeks to protect her daughter from evil glances by placing a little bread and salt in her pocket; and when a young girl goes out for a walk the mother sprinkles salt on the ground behind her, so that she may not lose her way.

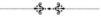

Holy water has been employed in the religious ceremonies of many peoples as a means of purifying both persons and things, and also to keep away demons. Sprinkling and washing with it were important features of the Greek ritual.

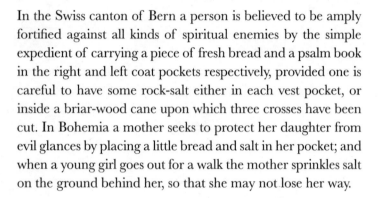

The holy water of the Roman Catholic Church is prepared by exorcising and blessing salt and water separately, after which the salt is dissolved in the water and a benediction pronounced upon the mixture. In the Hawaiian ritual, seawater was sometimes preferred.

A Magyar house-mistress will not give any salt to a woman who may come to the door and ask for it in the early morning, believing that any such would-be borrower is surely a witch; but in order to keep away all witches and hags, she strews salt on the threshold. On St Lucien's Day neither salt nor fire must be taken out of the house.

Among the Japanese, the mysterious preservative qualities of salt are the source of various superstitions. The mistress of a household will not buy it at night, and when purchased in the daytime a small quantity is thrown into the fire in order to prevent discord in the family, and to avert misfortune generally.

In Scotland salt was formerly in high repute as a charm, and the salt-box was the first chattel to be removed to a new dwelling. When Robert Burns, in the year 1789, was about to occupy a new house at Ellisland, he was escorted on his route thither along the banks of the river Nith by a procession of relatives, and in their midst was borne a bowl of salt resting on the family Bible.

In some places in the north of England the giving away of salt is a dangerous procedure; for if the salt thus given comes into the possession of an evil-wisher, it places the donor entirely in the power of such a person.

In upper Egypt, previous to the setting out of a caravan, it is customary for the native women to throw salt on burning coals, which are carried in earthen vessels and set down before the different loads. While so doing they exclaim, 'May you be blessed in going and coming', and such incantations they believe render inert all the machinations of evil spirits.

# THE OMENS
# OF SNEEZING

*He is a friend at sneezing time; the most
that can be got from him is a 'God bless you'!*
– Italian proverb

## IN ANCIENT TIMES

The ancient Egyptians regarded the head as a citadel or
fortress in which the reasoning faculty abode. Hence they
especially revered any function seemingly appertaining to so
noble a portion of the body, and dignified even the insigni-
ficant act of sneezing by attributing to it auguries for good or
evil, according to the position of the moon with reference to
the signs of the zodiac.

---

The Greeks and Romans also, by whom the most trivial
occurrences of everyday life were thought to be omens of
good fortune or the reverse, considered the phenomena of
sneezing as not the least important in this regard. Homer
tells us in the Odyssey that the Princess Penelope, troubled
by the importunities of her suitors, prayed to the gods for
the speedy return of her husband Ulysses. Scarcely was her
prayer ended when her son Telemachus sneezed, and this

event was regarded by Penelope as an intimation that her petition would be granted.

———— ❧ ·• ❧ ————

Aristotle said that there was a god of sneezing, and that when in Greece any business enterprise was to be undertaken, two or four sneezes were thought to be favorable. If more than four, the auspices were indifferent, while one or three rendered it hazardous to proceed. About this, however, there appears to have been no unvarying rule. Sneezing at a banquet was considered by the Romans to be especially ominous; and when it unfortunately occurred, some of the viands were brought back to the table and again tasted, as this was thought to counteract any evil effects.

———— ❧ ·• ❧ ————

The Greeks considered that the brain controlled the function of sneezing. They were therefore as careful to avoid eating this portion of any animal as the Pythagoreans were to avoid beans as an article of diet.

———— ❧ ·• ❧ ————

It is related that just before the battle of Salamis, 480 BC, and while Themistocles, the Athenian commander, was offering a sacrifice to the gods on the deck of his galley, a sneeze was heard on the right hand, which was hailed as a fortunate omen by Euphrantides the Soothsayer.

———— ❧ ·• ❧ ————

Again, it happened once that while Xenophon was addressing his soldiers, referring to the righteousness of their cause and the consequent divine favor which might be expected, someone chanced to sneeze. Pausing in his address, the great general remarked that Jupiter had been pleased to send them a happy omen, and it seemed therefore but right to make an offering to the gods. Then, after all the company had joined in a hymn of thanksgiving, the sacrifice was made, and Xenophon continued with his exhortation.

———— ❧•❧ ————

Among the ancients sneezing to the right was considered fortunate and to the left unlucky. In some erotic verses with the title 'Acme and Septimius', by the Roman poet Catullus, are these lines, twice repeated:

> *Love stood listening with delight,*
> *And sneezed his auspice on the right.*

———— ❧•❧ ————

The omens of sneezing were thought to be of especial significance in lovers' affairs, and indeed the classic poets were wont to say of beautiful women that Love had sneezed at their birth. The Italian poet, Propertius, while asserting his enduring affection for Cynthia, the daughter of the poet Hostius, thus apostrophizes the chief theme of his eulogies: 'In thy newborn days, my life, did golden Love sneeze loud and clear a favoring omen.'

———— ❧•❧ ————

The Egyptians, Greeks, and Romans regarded the act of sneezing as a kind of divinity or oracle, which warned them on various occasions as to the course they should pursue, and also foretold future good or evil.

Plutarch said that the familiar spirit or demon of Socrates was simply the sneezing either of the philosopher himself or of those about him. If any person in his company sneezed on his right hand, Socrates felt encouraged to proceed with the project or enterprise which he may have had in mind. But if the sneeze were on his left hand, he abandoned the undertaking.

If he himself sneezed when he was doubtful whether or not to do anything, he regarded it as evidence in the affirmative; but if he happened to sneeze after any work was already entered upon, he immediately desisted therefrom. The demon, we are told, always notified him by a slight sneeze whenever his wife Xantippe was about to have a scolding fit, so that he was thus enabled opportunely to absent himself. And in so doing Socrates appears to have given proof, were any needed, of his superior wisdom; for Xantippe had been known to upset the supper table in her anger, and that, too, when a guest was present.

On a column in the garden of the House of the Faun, at Pompeii, there is a Latin inscription which may be freely translated as follows: 'Victoria, good luck to thee and wherever thou wilt, sneeze pleasantly.'

Clement of Alexandria, in a treatise on politeness, characterizes sneezing as effeminate and as a sign of intemperance.

Probably the only Biblical reference to the subject of sneezing is in 2 Kings 4:35, where the son of the Sbunamite sneezed seven times and then revived at the prayer of Elisha.

Horapollo, in his treatise on Egyptian hieroglyphics, says that the inhabitants of ancient Egypt believed that the capacity for sneezing was in inverse ratio to the size of the spleen; and they portrayed the dog as the personification of sneezing and smelling, because they believed that that animal had a very small spleen. On the other hand, they held that animals with large spleens were unable to sneeze, smell, or laugh, that is, to be open, blithe, or frank-hearted.

The function of the spleen in the animal economy is not fully understood today. If the above theory were correct, we should expect that the removal of a dog's spleen would incite excessive sternutation and render more acute the sense of smell, whereas the only marked result of the operation is a voracious appetite. The theory is certainly unique, as well as illogical and absurd.

St Augustine wrote that, in his time, so prevalent was faith in the omens of sneezing that a man would return to bed if he happened to sneeze while putting on his shoes in the morning.

The learned English prelate, Alcuin (735–804), expressed the opinion that sneezings were devoid of value as auguries except to those who placed reliance in them. But he further remarked that 'it was permitted to the evil spirit, for the deceiving of persons who observe these things, to cause that in some degree prognostics should often foretell the truth.'

In an ancient Anglo-Saxon sermon, a copy of which is in the library of Cambridge University, England, reference is made to certain superstitions existing among the Saxons before their conversion to Christianity. The writer says; 'Everyone who trusts in divinations, either by fowls or by sneezings, or by horses or dogs, he is no Christian, but a notorious apostate.'

## MODERN SUPERSTITIONS ABOUT SNEEZING

Sneezing at the commencement of an undertaking, whether it be an important enterprise or the most commonplace act, has usually been accounted unlucky. Thus, according to a modern Teutonic belief, if a man sneeze on getting up in the morning, he should lie down again for another three hours, else his wife will be his master for a week. So likewise the pious Hindu, who may perchance sneeze while beginning his morning ablutions in the river Ganges, immediately recommences his prayers and toilet; and among the Alfoorans or aborigines of the island of Celebes in the Indian archipelago, if one happens to sneeze when about leaving a gathering of friends, he at once resumes his seat for a while before making another start.

---

When a native of the Banks Islands, in Polynesia, sneezes, he imagines that someone is calling his name, either with good or evil intent, the motive being shown by the character of the sneeze. Thus a gentle sneeze implies kindly feeling on the part of the person speaking of him, while a violent paroxysm indicates a malediction.

In the latter case he resorts to a peculiar form of divination in order to ascertain who it is that curses him. This consists in raising the arms above the head and revolving the closed fists one around the other. The revolution of the fists is the question, 'Is it such an one?' Then the arms are thrown out, and the answer, presumably affirmative, is given by the cracking of the elbow joints.

---

In Scotland even educated people have been known to maintain that idiots are incapable of sneezing, and hence, if this be true, the inference is clear that the act of sternutation is *prima facie* evidence of the possession of a certain degree of intelligence.

British nurses used to think that infants were under a fairy spell until they sneezed. 'God sain the bairn', exclaimed an old Scotch nurse when her little charge sneezed at length, 'it's no a warlock'.

The Irish people also entertain similar beliefs. Thus in Lady Wilde's *Ancient Cures, Charms, and Usages of Ireland* is to be found the following description of a magical ceremony for the cure of a fairy-stricken child. A good fire is made, wherein is thrown a quantity of certain herbs prescribed by the fairy women; and after a thick smoke has risen, the child is carried thrice around the fire while an incantation is repeated and holy water is sprinkled about liberally. Meantime all doors must be closed, lest some inquisitive fairy enter and spy upon the proceedings; and the magical rites must be continued until the child sneezes three times, for this looses the spell, and the little one is permanently redeemed from the power of witches.

Among uncivilized peoples the sneeze of a young child has a certain mystic significance, and is intimately associated with its prospective welfare or ill-luck. When, therefore, a Maori infant sneezes, its mother immediately recites a long charm of words. If the sneeze occurs during a meal, it is thought to be prognostic of a visit, or of some interesting piece of news; whereas in Tonga it is deemed an evil token.

So, too, among the New Zealanders, if a child sneeze on the occasion of receiving its name, the officiating priest at once holds to its ear the wooden image of an idol and sings some mystic words.

In a note appended to his 'Mountain Bard', the Ettrick Shepherd says, regarding the superstitions of Selkirkshire: 'When they sneeze in first stepping out of bed in the morning, they are thence certified that strangers will be there in the course of the day, in numbers corresponding to the times they sneeze.'

It was a Flemish belief that a sneeze during a conversation proved that what one said was the truth, a doctrine which must have commended itself to snuff-takers.

In Shetlandic and Welsh folklore the sneeze of a cat indicates cold north winds in summer and snow in winter; and the Bohemians have an alleged infallible test for recognizing the Devil, for they believe that he must perforce sneeze violently at sight of a cross.

According to a Chinese superstition a sneeze on New Year's Eve is ominous for the coming year; and, to offset this, the sneezer must visit three families of different surnames, and beg from each a small tortoise-shaped cake, which must be eaten before midnight.

In Turkistan, when a person to whom a remark is addressed sneezes, it is an asseveration that the opinion or statement is correct, just as if the person accosted were to exclaim, 'That is true!' In the same country three sneezes are unlucky. When, also, anyone hiccoughs, it is etiquette to say, 'You stole something from me,' and this phrase at such times is supposed to produce good luck.

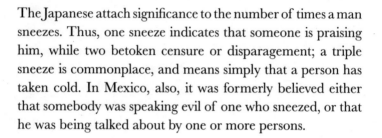

The Japanese attach significance to the number of times a man sneezes. Thus, one sneeze indicates that someone is praising him, while two betoken censure or disparagement; a triple sneeze is commonplace, and means simply that a person has taken cold. In Mexico, also, it was formerly believed either that somebody was speaking evil of one who sneezed, or that he was being talked about by one or more persons.

Sussex people are prejudiced against cats which develop sneezing proclivities, for they believe that, when a pet feline sneezes thrice, it augurs ill for the health of the household, and is premonitory of influenza and bronchial affections.

# THE DOCTRINE OF DEMONIACAL POSSESSION

The natural instinct of the untutored is to regard the act of sneezing as the manifestation of an attack by a demon.

Certain African tribes, for instance, are said to believe that whoever sneezes is possessed of an evil spirit, to whose malicious agency is due the violence of the paroxysm and its utter disregard of times and seasons.

———— ❧ • ❧ ————

Dr Edward B. Tylor asserts that the Zulus have faith in the agency of kindly spirits as well, and says that, when one of these people sneezes, he is wont to exclaim: 'I am now blessed; the ancestral spirit is with me. Let me hasten and praise it, for it is that which causes me to sneeze.' Thereupon he praises the spirits of the dead, and asks for various blessings. But among most uncivilized peoples sneezing is placed in the category of paroxysmal diseases, and reckoned to be of demoniac origin.

Inasmuch as sneezing is often one symptom of an incipient cold, which is a physical ailment, and as among tribes every physical ailment is regarded as a case of demoniacal possession, the use of charms and exorcisms to counteract the efforts of the evil spirits seems a natural expedient.

———— ❧ • ❧ ————

When an American Indian falls sick, he believes his illness to be the work of some spiteful demon. Therefore, when he gets well, he changes his name, so that the demon may not be able to recognize him again.

———— ❧ • ❧ ————

The chief aim of the medicine man, in treating a patient, is the expulsion of the evil spirit; and this is the prime object of the various superstitious ceremonies and incantations which are a prominent feature in medical practice among savages. The medicine man strives to drive away the demon by frightful sounds and gesticulations, and by hideous grimaces and contortions. Sometimes he makes a small image typifying the spirit of sickness, and this image is then maliciously broken in pieces.

---

The natives of West Africa believe that the mere mention of unpleasant names suffices to frighten away the demons who cause sickness; and these spirits may moreover be deceived by simply changing the name of a sick child. In the province of Tonquin, a French possession in south-eastern Asia, hateful names given to ailing children are likewise thought to terrify the evil spirits; but when the little patients are convalescent, pleasanter names are substituted.

---

The Indians of Nootka Sound, Vancouver Island, attribute physical ailments either to the absence or irregular conduct of the soul, or to the agency of spirits, and medical practice is governed accordingly; therefore the Okanogons of the State of Washington subject patients affected with serious illnesses to the magical treatment of the medicine man.

---

The islanders of the South Pacific have their own doctrine about the philosophy of sneezing. They believe that, when the spirit goes traveling about, its return naturally occasions some commotion, as is evident from the violent act of sneezing. They therefore deem it proper to welcome back the wandering spirit, the form of greeting varying in the different islands. The phrase employed by the natives of Raratonga, for example, means 'Ha! You have come back!'

———— ❖ • ❖ ————

The 'Sadda', one of the sacred books of the Parsees, counsels the faithful to have recourse to prayer when they sneeze, because at that critical moment the demon is especially active.

The Parsees regard sneezing as a manifestation that the evil spirits, who are constantly seeking to enter the body, have been forcibly expelled by the interior fire which, in their belief, animates every human being. When, therefore, a Parsee hears anyone sneeze, he exclaims, 'Blessed be Ormuzd!' thus praising his chief deity. The Parsees are forbidden to talk while eating, because at such times demons are on the alert, watching for opportunities to gain admission to the body through the mouth while a person is engaged in conversation.

———— ❖ • ❖ ————

Pious Brahmins are careful to touch the right ear when they happen to sneeze either during the performance of a religious ceremony or at certain other times specified in the 'Shastra', or holy books of the Hindus. Evil spirits were believed to enter the body through the ears, as well as by the nose or mouth, and the object of touching the ear was to prevent their gaining admission there.

———— ❖ • ❖ ————

The natives of Turkistan consider yawning to be a repre-
hensible act, originating from an evil place in one's heart,
and indicative of a state of preparedness for the reception
of demons. When, therefore, they yawn, the hand is placed,
palm outwards, before the open mouth, thus barring out the
demons.

---

The once popular opinion, which is still met with today, that
the efficacy of a medicine is proportionate to its harshness
of flavor, is probably a relic of the ancient theory which
attributed illnesses to possession by evil spirits. When one's
body was believed to be the abode of such a spirit, the natural
desire was to drive out the unwelcome visitor, and to force him
to seek some other habitation. Nowadays we have so far abandoned this theory that, while we may have faith in the virtues
of bitter herbs, we are ready to welcome also the palatable
remedies of the modern pharmacopoeia; but until comparatively recent times the science of therapeutics was dominated
by superstition, and physicians prescribed remedies composed
of the most repulsive and uncanny ingredients.

---

In Tibet antiseptics are employed in surgical operations, the
rationale of their use in that country being the preservation
of the wound from evil spirits; and when smallpox rages in
the neighborhood of the city of Leh, capital of the province
of Ladakh, the country people seek to ward off the epidemic
by placing thorns on their bridges and at their boundary lines.

    This practice is strikingly analogous in principle to some of
the superstitious uses of iron and steel in the form of sharp

instruments, of which mention has been made elsewhere in this volume.

The aboriginal Tibetans ascribe illnesses to the spite of demons, and hence a chief object of their religious rites is the pacification of these malignant beings by the sacrifice of a cow, pig, goat, or other animal.

Throughout Christendom it is customary for those present to invoke the divine blessing upon a person who sneezes, and the Muslim, under like circumstances, prays to Allah for aid against the powers of evil. In either case the underlying idea appears to be the same, namely, the doctrine of invading spirits.

In ancient Egypt illnesses were thought to be caused by demons who had somehow entered the patient's body and taken up their abode there; and the Chaldean physicians, actuated by the same belief, were wont to prescribe the most nauseating medicines in order to thoroughly disgust the demon in possession, and thus enforce his departure.

This doctrine of spiritual possession was formerly even supposed to be warranted by Scripture, and especially by a verse of the 141st Psalm: 'Set a watch, Lord, before my mouth; keep the door of my lips.' This passage was interpreted as an entreaty for preservation from evil spirits, who were likely to enter the body through the mouth, especially during the acts of yawning, sneezing, talking, and eating. The Hindus consider yawning as dangerous for this reason, and hence the practice of mouth-washing, which is a part of their daily ritual. Hence also their custom of cracking their fingers and exclaiming 'Great God!' after yawning, to intimidate the *Bhúts*, or malignant spirits. Sneezing is usually accounted lucky in India, except at the commencement of an undertaking, because it means the expulsion of a *Bhút*.

Josephus relates having seen a Jew named Eleazar exorcise devils from people who were possessed, in the presence of the Emperor Vespasian and many of his soldiers. His mode of procedure consisted in applying to the demoniac's nose a ring containing a piece of the root of a magical herb, and then withdrawing the evil spirit through the nostrils, meanwhile repeating certain incantations originally composed by Solomon.

## SALUTATION AFTER SNEEZING

The origin of the benediction after sneezing, a custom well-nigh universal, is involved in obscurity. A popular legend says that, before the time of Jacob, men sneezed but once, as the shock proved fatal. The patriarch, however, obtained by intercession a relaxation of this law, on condition that every sneeze should be consecrated by an ejaculatory prayer. According to a well-known myth of classical antiquity, Prometheus formed of clay the model of a man, and desiring to animate the lifeless figure, was borne to heaven by the Goddess Minerva, where he filled a reed with celestial fire stolen from a wheel of the Sun's chariot. Returning then to earth, he applied the magical reed to the nostrils of the image, which thereupon became a living man, and began its existence by sneezing. Prometheus, delighted with his success, uttered a fervent wish for the welfare of his newly formed creature. The latter thenceforward always repeated aloud the same benediction whenever he heard anyone sneeze, and enjoined upon his children the same practice, which was thus transmitted to succeeding generations.

---

Famianus Strada, the Italian Jesuit historian (1572–1649), in his *Prolusiones Academicae*, relates that one day, when Cicero was present at a performance of the Roman opera, he began to sneeze, whereupon the entire audience, irrespective of rank, arose and with one accord cried out, 'God bless you!' or, as the common phrase was, 'May Jupiter be with thee!' Whereat three young men named Fannius, Fabalus, and Lemniscus, who were lounging in one of the boxes, began an animated discussion in regard to the antiquity of this custom, which all believed to have originated with Prometheus.

---

Even in the time of Aristotle, salutation after sneezing was considered an ancient custom; and references to it are to be found in the writings of Roman authors. Pliny narrates in his *Natural History* that the Emperor Tiberius Caesar, who was known as one of the most melancholy and unsociable of men, scrupulously exacted a benediction from his attendants whenever he sneezed, whether in his palace or while driving in his chariot; and Apuleius, the platonic philosopher of the second century, alludes to the subject in his story of 'The Fuller's Wife'.

---

Although the fact of the existence of this custom centuries before the Christian era is beyond cavil, yet a very general popular belief attributes its origin to a much later period. The Italian historian, Carlo Sigonio, voices this belief in his statement that the practice began in the sixth century, during the pontificate of Gregory the Great. At this period a virulent pestilence raged in Italy, which proved fatal to those who sneezed. The Pope, therefore, ordered prayers to be said against it, accompanied by certain signs of the cross. And the people were wont also to say to those who sneezed, 'God help ye!' a revival of a custom dating back to prehistoric times.

The Icelander, when he sneezes, says, 'God help me!' and to another person who sneezes he says, 'God help you!' In Icelandic tradition the custom dates from a remote period, when the Black Pest raged virulently in portions of the country, and the mortality therefrom was great. At length the scourge reached a certain farm where lived a brother and sister, and they observed that the members of the household who succumbed to the disease were first attacked by a violent paroxysm of sneezing; therefore they were wont to exclaim 'God help me!' when they themselves sneezed.

Of all the inhabitants of that district, these two were the only ones who survived the pest, and hence the Icelanders, throughout succeeding generations, have continued the pious custom thus originated.

In mediaeval German poetry are to be found occasional references to this subject, as in the following passage quoted in Grimm's *Teutonic Mythology*: 'The pagans durst not sneeze, even though one should say, "God help thee".' And in the same work allusion is made to a quaint bit of fairy-lore about enchanted sprites sneezing under a bridge, that someone may call out 'God help', and undo the spell.

———❖••❖———

In the year 1542 the Spanish explorer, Hernando de Soto, received a visit in Florida from a native chief named Guachoya, and during their interview the latter sneezed. Immediately his attendants arose and saluted him with respectful gestures, at the same time saying: 'May the Sun guard thee, be with thee, enlighten thee, magnify thee, protect thee, favor thee', and other similar good wishes. And the Spaniards who were present were impressed by the fact that, in connection with sneezing, even more elaborate ceremonies were observed by savage tribes than those which obtained among civilized nations. And hence they reasoned that such observances were natural and instinctive with all mankind. We have the testimony of the earliest English explorers that the custom of salutation after sneezing was common in the remotest portions of Africa and in the Far East. Speke and Grant were unable to discover any trace of religion among the natives of equatorial Africa, except in their practice of uttering an Arabic ejaculation or prayer whenever a person sneezed.

———❖••❖———

The Portuguese traveler, Godinho, wrote that whenever the emperor of Monomotapa sneezed, acclamations were universal throughout his realm; and in Guinea in the last century, whenever a person of rank sneezed, everyone present knelt down, clapped their hands, and wished him every blessing. The courtiers of the king of Sennaar in Nubia are wont on the occasion of a royal sneeze to turn their backs on their sovereign while vigorously slapping the right hip. Among the Zulu tribes, sneezing is viewed as a favorable symptom in a sick person, and the natives are accustomed to return thanks after it. In Madagascar, when a child sneezes, its mother invokes the divine blessing, conformably to European usage; and in Persia the sneezer is the recipient of congratulations and good wishes.

—————�֍·ᴥ·✮—————

In the 'Zend-Avesta', or sacred writings of the Persian religion, is the injunction: 'And whensoever it be that thou hearest a sneeze given by thy neighbor, thou shalt say unto him, Ahunavar Ashim-Vuhu, and so shall it be well with thee.' In Egypt, if a man sneeze, he says, 'Praise be to God!' and all present, with the exception of servants, rejoin, 'God have mercy upon you!'

—————✖·ᴥ·✮—————

The Omahas, Dakotas, and other Sioux tribes of American Indians attach a peculiar importance to sneezing. Thus, if one of their number sneeze once, he believes that his name has been called either by his son, his wife, or some intimate friend. Hence he at once exclaims, 'My son!' But if he sneeze twice, he says, 'My son and his mother!'

—————✖·ᴥ·✮—————

In France the rules of etiquette formerly required that a gentleman who sneezed in the presence of another should take off his hat, and on the subsidence of the paroxysm he was expected formally to return the salutes of all present. The salutation of sneezers by removal of the hat was customary in England also. Joseph Hall, who was Bishop of Exeter in 1627, wrote that when a superstitious man sneezed he did not reckon among his friends those present who failed to uncover.

———————❖••❖———————

The Italians are wont to salute the sneezer with the ejaculation *Viva* or *Felicità*; and it has been reasoned that the latter expression may have been sometimes employed under like circumstances by the ancient Romans, because an advertisement on the walls of Pompeii concludes by wishing the people Godspeed with the single word *Felicitas!*

———————❖••❖———————

So, too, in Ireland the sneezer is greeted with fervent benedictions, such as, 'The blessing of God and the holy Mary be upon you!' for such invocations are thought to counteract the machinations of evil-disposed fairies.

———————❖••❖———————

The Siamese have a unique theory of their own on this subject. They believe that the Supreme Judge of the spiritual world is continually turning over the pages of a book containing an account of the life and doings of every human being; and when he comes to the page relating to any individual, the latter never fails to sneeze. In this way the Siamese endeavor to give a plausible reason for the prevalence of sneezing among men, and also for the accompanying salutation. In Siam and Laos the ordinary expression is, 'May the judgment be favorable to you.'

In the Netherlands a person who sneezes is believed thereby to place himself in the power of a witch, unless someone invokes a divine blessing; and such notions afford a plausible explanation of one theory of the origin of this custom.

Grimm refers to a passage in the 'Avadanas', or Buddhist parables, in which the rat is represented as wishing the cat joy when she sneezes. And in the department of Finistère in northwest France, when a horse sneezes or coughs the people say, 'May St Eloy assist you!' St Eloy was the guardian of farriers and the tutelar god of horses.

The natives of the Fiji Islands exclaim after a sneeze, '*Mbula*', that is, 'May you live!' or 'Health to you!' And the sneezer politely responds with '*Mole*', 'Thanks'. Formerly Fijian etiquette was yet more exacting and required the sneezer to add, 'May you club someone!' or 'May your wife have twins!'

A Spanish writer, Juan Cervera Bachiller, in his book *Creencias y superstitiones*, Madrid, 1883, says that this widely diffused practice appears to have originated partly from religious motives and partly from gallantry, and that it is as obviously a relic of pagan times as are the various omens which have ever been associated with sneezing.

The apparently independent origin of the custom of salutation after sneezing among nations remote from each other, and its prevalence from time immemorial alike in the most cultured communities and among uncivilized races, have been thought to furnish striking evidence of the essential similarity of human minds, whatever their environment.

# DAYS OF GOOD AND EVIL OMEN

*Friday's moon,*
*Come when it will,*
*it comes too soon.*
– Proverb

## EGYPTIAN DAYS

The belief in lucky and unlucky days appears to have been first taught by the magicians of ancient Chaldea, and we learn from history that similar notions affected every detail of primitive Babylonian life, thousands of years before Christ. Reference to an 'unlucky month' is to be found in a list of deprecatory incantations contained in a document from the library of the royal palace at Nineveh. This document is written in the Accadian dialect of the Turanian language, which was akin to that spoken in the region of the lower Euphrates; a language already obsolete and unintelligible to the Assyrians of the seventh century BC. Certain days were called *Dies Egyptiaci*, because they were thought to have been pronounced unlucky by the astrologers of ancient Egypt.

In that country the unlucky days were, however, fewer in number than the fortunate ones, and they also differed in the degree of their ill-luck. Thus, while some were markedly ominous, others merely threatened misfortune, and still others were of mixed augury, partly good and partly evil. There were certain days upon which absolute idleness was enjoined upon the people, when they were expected to sit quietly at home, indulging in *dolce far niente*.

---

The poet Hesiod, who is believed to have flourished about one thousand years BC, in the third book of his poem, 'Works and Days', which is indeed a kind of metrical almanac, distinguishes lucky days from others, and gives advice to farmers regarding the most favorable days for the various operations of agriculture. Thus he recommends the eleventh of the month as excellent for reaping corn, and the twelfth for shearing sheep. But the thirteenth was an unlucky day for sowing, though favorable for planting. The fifth of each month was an especially unfortunate day, while the thirtieth was the most propitious of all.

---

Some of the most intelligent and learned Greeks were very punctilious in their observance of Egyptian days. The philosopher Proclus was said to be even more scrupulous in this regard than the Egyptians themselves. And Plotinus, another eminent Grecian philosopher, believed with the astrologers of a later day, that the positions of the planets in the heavens exerted an influence over human affairs.

---

In an ancient calendar of the year 334, in the reign of Constantine the Great, twenty-six Egyptian days were

designated. At an early period, however, the church authorities forbade the superstitious observance of these days.

---

Some of the most eminent early writers of the Christian
Church, St Ambrose, St Augustine, and St Chrysostom,
were earnest in their denunciation of the prevalent custom
of regulating the affairs of life by reference to the supposed
omens of the calendar. The fourth council of Carthage, in
398, censured such practices; and the synod of Rouen, in
the reign of Clovis, anathematized those who placed faith in
such relics of paganism.

---

We learn on the authority of Marco Polo that the Brahmins
of the province of Laristan, in southern Persia, in the thirteenth century, were extremely punctilious in their choice of
suitable days for the performance of any business matters.
This famous traveler wrote that a Brahmin who contemplated
making a purchase, for example, would measure the length
of his own shadow in the early morning sunlight, and if the
shadow were of the proper length, as officially prescribed for
that day, he would proceed to make the purchase; otherwise
he would wait until the shadow conformed in length to a
predetermined standard for that day of the week.

---

The Latin historian Rolandino in the third book of his
*Chronicle*, describes an undertaking which resulted disastrously
because, as was alleged, it was rashly begun on an 'Egyptian

day'. There is frequent mention of these days in many ancient manuscripts in the Ambrosian Library at Milan.

---

In a so-called 'Book of Precedents', printed in 1616, fifty-three days are specified as being 'such as the Egyptians noted to be dangerous to begin or take anything in hand, or to take a journey or any such thing'. An ancient manuscript mentions 'twenty-eight days in the year which were revealed by the Angel Gabriel to good Joseph, which ever have been remarked to be very fortunayte dayes either to let blood, cure wounds, use marchandizes, sow seed, build houses, or take journees.'

---

Astrologers formerly specified particular days when it was dangerous for physicians to bleed patients; and especially to be avoided were the first Monday in April, on which day Cain was born and his brother Abel slain; the first Monday in August, the alleged anniversary of the destruction of Sodom and Gomorrah; and the last Monday in December, which was the reputed birthday of Judas Iscariot.

---

In Mason's *Anatomie of Sorcerie* (1612), the prevailing notions on this subject were characterized as vain speculations of the astrologers, having neither foundation in God's word nor yet natural reason to support them, but being grounded only upon the superstitious imagination of men. A work of 1620, entitled *Melton's Astrologaster*, says that the Christian faith is violated when, like a pagan and apostate, any man 'doth observe those days which are called Egyptiaci, or the calends of January, or any month, day, time, or year, either to travel, marry or do anything in.' And the learned Sir Thomas Browne, in his *Pseudodoxia Epidemica*, published in 1658, declaimed in quaint but forcible language against the frivolity of such doctrines.

# ROMAN SUPERSTITION CONCERNING DAYS

The Romans had their *dies fasti*, corresponding to the modern court days in England. On such days, of which there were thirty-eight in the year, it was lawful for the praetor to administer justice and to pronounce the three words, *Do, dico, addico*, 'I give laws, declare right, and adjudge losses.'

The days on which the courts were not held were called nefasti (from *ne* and *fari*), because the three words could not then be legally spoken by the praetor. But these days came to be regarded as unlucky, a fact rendered evident by an expression of Horace. The Romans also classed as unfortunate the days immediately following the calends, nones, and ides of each month. Unlucky days were termed *dies atri*, because they were marked in the calendar with black charcoal, the lucky ones being indicated by means of white chalk. There were also days which were thought especially favorable for martial operations, but the anniversary of a national misfortune was considered very inauspicious. Thus after the defeat of the Romans by the Gauls under Brennus on the banks of the river Allia, July 16, 390 BC, that date was given a prominent place among the black days of the calendar. But not every general was influenced by such superstitions. Lucullus, when an attempt was made to dissuade him from attacking Tigranes, king of Armenia (whom he defeated 69 BC), because upon that date the Cimbri had vanquished a Roman army, replied, 'I will make it a day of *good* omen for the Romans.' The Roman ladies, we are told, gave less heed to the unlucky days of their own calendar than to the works of Egyptian astrologers, among whom Petosiris was their favorite authority, when they wished to ascertain the proper day, and even the hour, for the performance of household and other duties.

⁂

Horace thus apostrophizes a tree, by whose fall he narrowly escaped being crushed at Sabinum: 'Thou cursed tree! Whoever he was that first planted thee did it surely on an unlucky day, and with a sacrilegious hand.'

⁂

The Latin writer, Macrobius, stated that when one of the *nundinoi* or market days fell upon New Year's, it was considered very unfortunate. In such an event the Emperor Augustus, who was very superstitious, adopted the method of inserting an extra day in the previous year and subtracting one from that ensuing, thus preserving the regularity of the Julian style of reckoning time. Ordinarily, however, New Year's Day was deemed auspicious, and on that day, as now, people were accustomed to wish each other happiness and good fortune.

⁂

# MODERN BELIEFS
# IN DAY FATALITY

Among the Chinese of today, as with the inhabitants of ancient Babylon, the days which are deemed favorable or otherwise for business transactions, farming operations, or for traveling are still determined by astrologers, and are indicated in an official almanac published annually at Peking by the Imperial Board of Astronomers. The various tribes of the island of Madagascar also are exceedingly superstitious in regard to the luck or ill-luck attending certain days, and the lives of children born at an unlucky time are sometimes sacrificed to save them from anticipated misfortune.

---

Natives of the Gold Coast of West Africa, in their divisions of the year, observe a 'long time' consisting of nineteen lucky days, and a 'short time' of seven equally propitious days. The seven days intervening between these two periods are considered unlucky, and during this time they undertake no voyages nor warlike enterprises. Somewhat similar ideas prevail in Java and Sumatra, and in many of the smaller islands of the Malay Archipelago.

---

The Cossacks of western Siberia, the natives of the Baltic provinces of the Russian Empire, and the Laplanders of the far North, all adapt their lives to the black and white days of their calendar.

———— ❖ • ❖ ————

The peasantry of West Sussex in England will not permit their children to go blackberrying on the tenth day of October, on account of a belief that the Devil goes afield on that day, and bad luck would surely befall anyone rash enough to eat fruit gathered under such circumstances. The same people believe that all cats born in the month of May are hypochondriacs, and have an unpleasant habit of bringing snakes and vipers into the house.

———— ❖ • ❖ ————

Among the Muslims of India there are in each month seven evil days, on which no enterprise is to be undertaken on any consideration. Some of the peculiar superstitions of these people with regard to traveling on the different week-days are shown in *Zanoon-E- Islam, or the Customs of the Mussulmans of India*, by Jaffur Shurreef. Thus, if anyone proposes journeying on Saturday, he should eat fish before starting, in order that his plan may be successfully accomplished, but on Sunday betel-leaf is preferable for this purpose. In like manner, on Monday he should look into a mirror in order to obtain wealth. On Tuesday he should eat coriander seed, and on Wednesday should partake of curdled milk before starting. On Thursday, if he eat raw sugar, he may confidently anticipate returning with plenty of merchandise; and on Friday, if he eat dressed meat, he will bring back pearls and jewels galore.

———— ❖ • ❖ ————

Some idea of the beliefs current in the mother country during the last century may be obtained by a study of the advertisements of astrologers and medical charlatans in the public press of that period. For example, in the year 1773 one Sylvester Partridge, proprietor and vendor of antidotes, elixirs, washes for freckles, plumpers for rounding the cheeks, glass eyes, calves and noses, ivory jaws, and a new receipt for changing the color of the hair, offered for a consideration to furnish advice as to the proper times and seasons for letting blood, and to indicate the most favorable aspect of the moon for drawing teeth and cutting corns. He proffered counsel, moreover, as to the avoidance of unlucky days for paring the nails, and the kindest zodiacal sign for grafting, inoculation, and opening of beehives.

---

In enlightened England there are still to be found many people who believe that the relative positions of the sun, moon, and planets are prime factors in determining the proper times and seasons for undertaking terrestrial enterprises. Zadkiel's *Almanac* for 1898 states that natural astrology is making good progress towards becoming once more a recognized science. To quote from the preface of this publication:

> As the whole body of the ocean is not able to keep down one single particle of free air, which must assuredly force its way to the surface to unite with the atmosphere, so cannot the combined forces of the prejudice and studied contempt of all the *soi-disant* 'really scientific men' of the end of the century prevent the truth of *astrologia sana* from soaring above their

futile efforts to crush it down, to join the great atmosphere of natural science, to enlighten the human mind in its onward course and effort, 'to soar through Nature up to Nature's God'.

One example may suffice to exhibit the character of the predictions given in this same work. Under the caption, 'Voice of the Stars', August 1898, the writer says that the stationary positions of Saturn and Uranus are likely to shake Spain (and perhaps Tuscany) physically and politically about the 10th or 11th insts. There will be strained diplomatic relations between the United States and Spain; for Mars in the sign Gemini, and Saturn in Sagittarius, must create friction and disturbances in both countries.

The Jewish current beliefs in the influence of certain days and seasons appear to have been mostly derived from the Romans of old. Even nowadays among the Jews no marriages are solemnized during the interval of fifty days between the Feast of the Passover and Pentecost; and formerly the favorite wedding days were those of the new or full moon. In Siam the 8th and 15th days of the moon are observed as sacred, and devoted to worship and rest from ordinary labor. Sportsmen are forbidden to hunt or fish on these days. The Siamese astrologers indicate the probable character of any year by associating it with some animal, upon whose back the New Year is represented as being mounted.

# THE SIXTH DAY
# OF THE WEEK

Let us now consider the subject of Friday as an alleged *dies mala*. The seven weekdays were originally named after Saturn, Jupiter, Mars, the Sun, Mercury, Venus, and the Moon, in the order given, and these names are found in the early Christian calendars. The Teutonic nations, however, adopted corresponding names in the Northern mythology – the Sun and Moon, Tyr, the Norse God of War, Wodan, Thor, Freyja, and Saturn; and our early Saxon ancestors worshiped images representing all these deities until Christianity supplanted paganism in Britain. It has been suggested that our Friday may have been named after Frigga, the wife of Odin and the principal goddess of the ancient Scandinavians. But it is much more probable that the day derives its name from Freyja, the Goddess of Love, a deity corresponding to the Roman Venus and the Grecian Aphrodite. Freyja, the most easily propitiated of the goddesses, was wont to listen favorably to all who invoked her aid, and was especially tender-hearted to disconsolate lovers. She dwelt in a magnificent palace, and journeyed about in a car drawn by two cats.

It has been hinted that Freyja's character was not irreproachable, and that thence arose Friday's ill-repute, but such an hypothesis is wholly untenable.

From the prose 'Edda' we learn that this goddess was the wife of one Odur, and had a daughter named Hnossa, who was wonderfully beautiful. Sad to relate, Freyja was abandoned by her husband, who went away to visit foreign lands, and she has since spent much time in weeping, her tears being turned into drops of pure gold.

The fish was an emblem of Freyja, and as such was offered by the Scandinavians to their goddess on the sixth day of the week. The fish was also held sacred by the Babylonians and Assyrians, and by the ancient Romans as a symbol of Venus.

---

The generally accepted theory is that the crucifixion of our Lord on Good Friday was the origin of the widespread superstitions regarding the sixth day of the week. It is highly probable, however, that these beliefs originated at a much earlier epoch; for similar ideas are current among the inhabitants of heathen countries, as in Hindustan, for example. According to an ancient monkish legend, Adam and Eve partook of the forbidden fruit on a Friday; and in the Middle Ages many inauspicious occurrences of history or tradition were thought to have happened on that day.

---

In a French manuscript of the year 1285, preserved in the Bibliotheque Nationale in Paris, entitled 'Recommandation du Vendredi', the following events are alleged to have occurred on a Friday: Adam's creation, his sin and expulsion from Eden, the murder of Abel, Christ's crucifixion, the stoning of Stephen, the massacre of the Innocents by Herod, the crucifixion of Peter, the beheading of Paul and that of John the Baptist, and the flight of the children of Israel through the Red Sea; also the Deluge, the Confusion of Tongues at the Tower of Babel, and the infliction of the Plagues upon the land of Egypt.

---

The following extract from a translation of a Saxon manuscript of about the year 1120 may serve to illustrate the credulity of that epoch in England, and the odium attaching to Friday:

> Whoever is born on Sunday or its night, shall live without anxiety and be handsome. If he is born on Monday or its night, he shall be killed of men, be he laic or be he cleric. If on Tuesday or its night, he shall be corrupt in his life, and sinful and perverse. If he be born on Wednesday or its night, he shall be very peaceable and easy and shall grow up well and be a lover of good... If he be born on Friday or its night, he shall be accursed of men, silly and crafty and loathsome to all men and shall ever be thinking evil in his heart, and shall be a thief and a great coward, and shall not live longer than to mid-age. If he is born on Saturday or its night, his deeds shall be renowned, he shall be an alderman, whether he be man or woman; many things shall happen unto him, and he shall live long.

———— ❖•❖ ————

Although the superstitions of the dark ages may seem to us so childish, it may yet be affirmed with reason that, in proportion to the enlightenment of the times, the beliefs then current regarding day-fatality were no more absurd than those of our own era. In the *Reliques of Ancient English Poetry*, by Thomas Percy, is to be found the following 'excellent way to get a fayrie':

First, get a broad square christall or Venice glasse, in length and breadth three inches. Then lay that glasse or christall in the blood of a white hen, three Wednesdayes or three Fridayes. Then take it out and wash it with holy aq; and fumigate it. Then take three hazle sticks or wands of an yeare groth; pill them fayre and white; and make them so longe as you write the spiritt's name, or fayrie's name, which you call three times on every stick being made flatt on one side. Then bury them under some hill, whereat you suppose fayries haunt, the Wednesday before you call her; and the Fridaye followinge take them uppe and at eight, or three or ten of the clocke which be good planetts and houres for that turne; but when you call be in cleane life and turn thy face towards the east, and when you have her bind her in that stone and glasse.

---

Whiston, the translator of Josephus, publicly proclaimed in London that the comet of 1712 would be visible on October 14 of that year, and that on the Friday morning ensuing the world would be destroyed by fire. In the resulting panic, many people embarked in boats on the Thames, believing the water to be the safer element, on that particular Friday at least.

---

Mr Charles Godfrey Leland, in his *Etruscan Roman Remains*, says that in certain mediaeval manuscripts the Goddess

Venus was represented as the Queen of Hearts and a dealer of lucky cards. Therefore Friday, the *Dies Veneris*, was sometimes considered a lucky day, especially for matrimony. This opinion finds favor in Glasgow, where a large proportion of marriages take place on this day; whereas, in the midland counties of England, less than two per cent of the weddings occur on the sixth day of the week.

---

References to the popular sentiment regarding Friday are frequent in the works of English writers. Sir Thomas Overbury, in his description of 'a faire and happy Milk-mayd', says: 'Her dreams are so chaste that shee dare tell them; only a Fridaie's dream is all her superstition: that she conceales for feare of anger.' Again, in the play of *Sir John Oldcastle* is this passage: 'Friday, quotha, a dismal day, Candlemas Day this year was Friday.' And in Scott's 'Marmion' is the following:

> *The Highlander, whose red claymore*
> *The battle turned on Maldas' shore,*
> *Will on a Friday morn look pale*
> *If asked to tell a fairy tale.*
> *He fears the vengeful Elfin King,*
> *Who leaves that day his grassy ring;*
> *Invisible to human ken,*
> *He walks among the sons of men.*

---

As a refreshing instance of independence of thought in a credulous age, we may quote from a letter written by Sir Winston Churchill, father of the Duke of Marlborough, and printed in a tract of 1687. The letter, though ungrammatical, is given verbatim:

> I have made great experience of the truth of it, and have set down Friday as my own lucky day, the day on which I was born, christened, married, and which, I believe, will be the day of my death. The day on which I have had sundry deliverances from perils by sea and land, perils by false brethren, perils of law suits, etc. I was knighted (by chance unexpected of myself) on the same day and have several good accidents happened to me on that day; and am so superstitious in the belief of its good omen, that I choose to begin any considerable action that concerns me, on the same day.

---

## FRIDAY IN MODERN TIMES

Friday is the Sabbath of the Muslims, corresponding to the Sunday of the Christians and the Saturday of the Jews. In Egypt Friday is therefore blessed above all other days, while Saturday is the most unfortunate.

---

However, although Friday was the day selected by Mahomet for the holding of the Muslim Assembly, it was not wholly devoted to religious worship, and at the conclusion of public prayers business was transacted as on any other week-day. Among Mohammedans Friday is considered the most lucky of days; and it is also the most popular for commencing any enterprise of importance, whether building a house, planting a garden, embarking on a voyage, contracting a marriage, or making a garment.

---

One reason for Mahomet's choice of Friday as the day for public prayers was probably because this day was consecrated by the people of many nations to Alilat, the celestial Venus or Urania, whom the ancient Arabs worshiped. Mahomet said that whoever bathed on Friday and walked to the public religious service, taking a seat near the Imam or Khalifah (the leader of a Muslim tribe), and listened attentively to the sermon, avoiding meanwhile frivolous conversation, would obtain the reward of a whole year's prayers at night for every step which he took between his home and the place of this assembly.

---

The Muslims among the peasants inhabiting the frontier region between Afghanistan and Hindustan have a special reverence for Friday; for they believe that on that day God rested, after having created the world. On Friday eve, according to their belief, the spirits of the departed are wont to revisit their former abodes, and hence the custom prevails of sending delicacies to the mosque at such times.

---

Friday was the most popular day for weddings among the Jews in mediaeval times, and its selection appears to have been due to expediency, because of its nearness to the Jewish Sabbath, and the convenience of associating the marriage ceremony with the services in the synagogue on the latter day. The bridal pair fasted on the morning of the wedding, and ashes were sprinkled over their heads during the ceremony.

According to the teachings of the Talmud, a second soul was believed to enter men's bodies every Friday evening and to remain throughout the following day, its presence being indicated by an increased appetite for food.

---

On Friday, says an old tradition, is held the Witches' Sabbath or Assembly, and one should be careful not to speak of these creatures on that day, for their hearing is then especially acute, and disrespectful remarks will render one liable to incur their spite.

---

In the popular belief of the Swabians, Friday is the day when the witches celebrate their joint festival with the Devil on the Heuberg, near Rotenburg, and afterward scour the country, intent on working all manner of mischief upon the people and their cattle.

---

According to a Scotch superstition, however, witches were supposed to hold their weekly meetings on Saturdays, in unfrequented places. The formal proceedings on these occasions included an address by the Devil, and the holding of a court, wherein each witch was expected to give a detailed statement of her doings; and those who had been idle were given a beating with their own broomsticks, the diligent being rewarded by gifts of enchanted bones. A dance followed, the Devil playing on the bag-pipes, and leading the music.

---

The Irish are careful not to mention fairies by name either on Wednesdays or Fridays, for these invisible creatures are unusually alert on these two days.

On Fridays especially, their power for evil is very strong. On that day, therefore, a careful watch is kept over the children and cattle; a lighted wisp of straw is waved about the baby's head, and a quenched coal is placed under the cradle and churn. And if the horses are more than usually restive in their stalls, it is a sure sign that the fairies are riding them; therefore the people spit three times at the animals, and the fairies thereupon immediately take their departure.

---

In Ireland Friday is *facile princeps* among unlucky days, and especial care should be taken not to open the door of one's dwelling to any stranger on that day. Neither butter nor milk should be given away, nor should a cat be taken from one house to another on a Friday. To undo a sorcerer's spell, one should eat barley cakes over which an incantation has been said; but the cakes must be eaten on a Monday or Thursday, and never on Friday.

---

In Welsh tradition the water-sprites are thought to keep an especially watchful eye over the sea on Fridays, making it rough and tempestuous.

On a Friday morning in the year 1600, says an old legend, a ship set sail from a Northern port, having on board a young man and a maiden of rare beauty, whose strange actions and demeanor seemed to betoken that they were supernatural beings. The vessel never reached port, but one stormy night a phantom ship was seen, enveloped in an uncanny light; and on its deck stood the youth and his sweetheart, a weird vision, as the spectral craft moved along over the stormy sea against the wind.

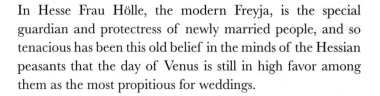

In Hesse Frau Hölle, the modern Freyja, is the special guardian and protectress of newly married people, and so tenacious has been this old belief in the minds of the Hessian peasants that the day of Venus is still in high favor among them as the most propitious for weddings.

In some places it is unlucky to receive any news, whether good or bad, on a Friday; and, according to a Shropshire saying, 'If you hear anything new on a Friday, it gives you another wrinkle on your face, and adds another year to your age.' Indeed, the term 'Friday-faced' was used to denote a gloomy or dejected visage, as in the following quotation: 'Marry, out upon him! What a friday-fac'd slave it is! I think in my conscience his face never keeps holiday.'

In Servia children born on Friday are thought to be invulnerable to the assaults of the whole army of hags and sorcerers.

In Germany Friday is reckoned the most fateful of all the week-days, whether for good or evil. The beliefs vary in different portions of the empire, but there is a universal prejudice against setting out on a journey, moving into a new house, or changing servants on this day.

In eastern Prussia, whoever bakes on a Friday will get but little bread; but Sunday baptisms are thought to offset the unlucky auspices of children born on Friday.

The North German farmers consider Friday the best day on which to begin gathering the harvest.

In olden times Friday was the most favorable day for courtship and weddings in Germany, and, unless a bride first entered her new home on that day, domestic strife was likely to ensue.

If she wished to tame a bad-tempered husband, her first care was to prepare for him a soup made with the rainwater of a Friday's shower. The magic charm of words wherewith cattle were freed from the mange was spoken on a Friday morning; and a hare which had been shot on the first Friday in March was of great therapeutic value, especially its eyes, which were dried and carried about as a sovereign remedy for defective vision.

---

Only on a Friday did the church bells strike the hour for the release of bewitched spirits, and the delivery of enchanted souls from their spells.

---

Doctor M. Hofler says that Bavarian peasants still cherish many superstitions about the sixth day of the week, the day sacred to Freyja, the old German Goddess of Love. Moreover, wonderful amuletic virtues are attributed to hens' eggs laid during Good Friday night, and whoever eats these eggs is thought to be thereby insured against bodily harm. How long this immunity holds good does not appear; but probably until another Good Friday night egg is eaten. In farmers' households these precious eggs are therefore eagerly sought by the house-mistress, who is wont to give them to her husband and the farm-hands; or else she uses them as an ingredient of the dough figures which ornament the Easter bread.

---

In some districts of Hungary the following peculiar custom is in vogue:

Whenever anyone's name-day happens on a Friday, that person selects a piece of one of his cast-off garments, rubs thereon a few drops of his own blood and saliva, and then burns the fragment of clothing. By so doing he burns up also all the ill luck which else might have befallen him during the next year. In south-eastern Transylvania a rag mystically dealt with as above is hung on a tree before sunrise on the day in question; if it disappear before dawn of the next day, the person who thus superstitiously celebrates the occurrence of his name-day on a Friday may laugh at ill luck for a year.

---

The Magyars begin no work on a Friday, for it is bound to miscarry; neither do they give any milk out of the house on that day, for by so doing they imagine the usefulness of the cow to be impaired. In Bihar County, Hungary, a loaf of bread baked on Friday and impaled upon a stick is accounted a safeguard against the spread of fire. The natives of this district likewise entertain various curious fancies which are decidedly unique. For example, when a newly born child is knock-kneed, the mother regards it as a changeling. She therefore seats herself on the threshold on a Tuesday or Friday, when witches are abroad, and peremptorily addresses those creatures, demanding the restoration of her own child, whom she believes they have stolen away. 'Pfui! Pfui! You scoundrels!' she exclaims, 'give it back!'

---

The Sicilians have a host of superstitions on this subject. The following are among the more interesting items of their folklore relating to Friday. On this day the owner of a rented house will not hand over the keys to a new tenant, neither would the latter receive them. In the southern part of the province of Palermo no thief dares steal on a Friday, and the accuracy of this statement is corroborated by the criminal statistics. Indeed, on this day the most timid house-holder may journey in safety anywhere in the province, a fact which the sagacious traveler in a land notorious for brigandage will not fail to note. This immunity is not attrib-utable to any special veneration for Freyja's day, but rather to a popular belief that thefts and other misdemeanors then committed are sure of speedy detection. Laughter is thought to offend the goddess, and the proverb runs, 'He who laughs on Friday weeps on Saturday.' In an anonymous manuscript in the municipal library of Palermo appears a statement that whoever cuts out garments on a Tuesday or a Friday runs the risk of making them too short and of losing the cloth. Such clothing has little wear in it, for nothing begun on these days has any durability.

---

The inhabitants of ancient Gascony are no less cred-ulous, as is apparent from the following bits of Friday lore. Anyone rash enough to start on a journey on horseback runs especial risk of falling off his horse, and of being drowned in attempting to ford a stream. It has even happened that newly baked loaves have been found tinged with blood in the oven.

However, Friday is a good day for making vinegar, and the casks filled at three o'clock in the afternoon of that day are found to be superior to others. This is because our Lord, while on the cross, was given vinegar to drink, mingled with gall, at three o'clock on the afternoon of Good Friday.

In Normandy, also, Friday is the favorite day for putting water in wine or cider, for the people believe that on any other day the mixture would become sour.

According to a quaint Italian belief, whoever is born on a Friday will be of sanguine temperament, passionate, light-hearted, and handsome. He will delight in music, both vocal and instrumental, and will have a liking for fine clothes. Moreover, he will be voluble in speech, though of unstable character.

The Tyrolese have a saying, 'Whoever is born on a Friday must experience trouble', and they regard it as folly to marry on that day.

The French people share fully the general distrust of the sixth day of the week. This is shown by statistics of the Parisian theatres, where there are produced on an average nearly 200 new pieces annually, and for many years not one of these has had its first performance on a Friday.

In Alsace Wednesday and Friday are unlucky days, and the former is never chosen for a wedding or baptism. But of the two, Friday is the more undesirable, and no business of importance is done thereon, nor any journey undertaken. It is foremost among witch days, for evil spirits are then abroad, and their activity on a Friday is proverbial. These sentiments prevail in other German districts, and are entertained by people of cultivation and learning.

———— ❧··❧ ————

Indeed, it may be affirmed truly that the possession of intellectual force is by no means incompatible with a superstitious belief in the luck or misfortune of particular days. The credulousness of the great Napoleon in this regard is well known. Bismarck is said to have once written to his wife from Letzlingen, a village of Prussian Saxony: 'I have not had such good luck in hunting today as I had three years ago; but then – it is a Friday.'

———— ❧··❧ ————

The French statesman, Gambetta, is reported to have arranged his journeyings and business affairs with reference to auspicious hours, as determined by a professional reader of cards; and President Felix Faure, we are told, is similarly credulous. Indeed, so prevalent are notions of this kind in the French capital that tastefully ornamented cards with a list of 'hours to be avoided' find a ready sale in the streets.

———— ❧··❧ ————

Among the Slavonians St Prascovia, the modern successor of Venus and Freyja, is believed to visit the peasants' houses every Friday, and woe to the luckless woman whom she then finds engaged in certain occupations. Local tradition says that sewing, spinning, and weaving on that day are sinful, and are especially distasteful to St Prascovia, familiarly known as 'Mother Friday', because the dust so produced gets into her eyes. She is very apt to take revenge by inflicting upon the offenders divers physical ailments, such as sore eyes, whitlows, or hang-nails. In some districts the peasants retire earlier than usual on Friday evenings, under the impression that Mother Friday will punish those whom she may find awake when she makes her evening visits. These popular beliefs are exemplified in the following tradition:

> There was once a certain woman who did not pay due reverence to Mother Friday, but set to work on a distaff full of flax, combing it and whirring it. She spun away until dinnertime, then sleep fell upon her. Suddenly the door opened, and in came Mother Friday, before the eyes of all who were there, clad in a white dress, and in such a rage! And she went straight up to the woman who had been spinning, and scooped up from the floor a handful of the dust that had fallen out of the flax, and began stuffing and stuffing that woman's eyes full of it! After she had stuffed them full, she went off in a rage – disappeared without saying a word.
>
> When the woman awoke, she began squalling, at the top of her voice, about her eyes, but could not tell what was the matter with them. The other women, who had been much frightened,

began to cry out: 'Oh, you wretch, you! You've brought a terrible punishment on yourself from Mother Friday.' Then they told her all that had taken place. She listened to it all, and then began imploring: 'Mother Friday, forgive me! Pardon me, the guilty one! I'll offer thee a taper, and I'll never let friend or foe dishonor thee, mother!'

Well, what do you think? During the night, back came Mother Friday, and took the dust out of that woman's eyes, so that she was able to get about again. It's a great sin to dishonor Mother Friday, combing and spinning flax, forsooth!

———— ⸙ • ⸙ ————

Professor Max Müller, in his 'Contributions to the Science of Mythology', cites a tradition of the as yet little known mythology of the Mordvinians, a Finnish race inhabiting the middle Volga provinces of Russia. A woman who had been working all day long on a Friday, baking bread for some orphan children, was taken up in a dream to the sun, and when she was nearly exhausted, owing to the effects of the heat, and to the rapidly increasing size of a piece of dough which she had put into her mouth, she was accosted by Chkaï, the large-eyed Mordvine sun-god, who told her that she was being punished because she had baked bread for the orphans on a Friday. She was charged, moreover, to tell all the people so. 'But who will be such a fool as to believe me?' asked the woman most disrespectfully. Thereupon Chkai placed his mark in scarlet and blue upon her forehead – an emblem which is thought to bring luck. And after that the Mordvine women were careful to bake no bread, nor to do any other work, on a Friday.

———— ◈ ◈ ————

It was a very early custom in England to appoint Friday as the day for the execution of criminals, and until recently the same was true in this country, but through the persistent efforts of the 'Thirteen Club', of New York, whose object is the discouragement of certain popular superstitions, the sixth day of the week has been partially relieved of the odium of being 'hangman's day' in the United States.

———— ◈ ◈ ————

A writer of an inventive turn of mind has suggested that Friday's unpopularity is partly owing to its being late in the week and money runs short to the poor. Saturday being the close of the week, and payday as well, there is no time then to be superstitious.

———— ◈ ◈ ————

Some modern writers have displayed a misguided zeal in the collection of statistical evidence that Friday has been a most auspicious day in American history, and have cited among other events the surrender of Burgoyne at Saratoga, and that of Cornwallis at Yorktown, as occurring on that day. But will such an argument appeal with success to English readers? If by general consent we should teach our children that Friday was the luckiest day of the week, evidence in favor of this theory would no doubt rapidly accumulate, and the new belief would soon be worth just as much as the old one.

———— ◈ ◈ ————

# SUPERSTITIOUS DEALINGS WITH ANIMALS

## RATS AND MICE AS AVENGERS

When in ancient times fields were overrun and crops destroyed by swarms of pestiferous animals or insects, these creatures were regarded either as agents of the Devil, or as being themselves veritable demons. We learn, moreover, that rats and mice were formerly especial objects of superstition, and that their actions were carefully noted as auguries of good or evil. A rabbinical myth says that the rat and the hog were created by Noah as scavengers of the Ark; but the rat becoming a nuisance, the patriarch evoked a cat from the lion's nose. In the *Horapollon*, the only ancient work now known which attempted to explain Egyptian hieroglyphics, the rat is represented as a symbol of destruction. But the Egyptians also regarded this animal as a type of good judgment, because, when afforded the choice of several pieces of bread, he always selects the best.

According to an early legend, the Teucri, or founders of the Trojan race, on leaving the island of Crete to found a colony elsewhere, were instructed by an oracle to choose as a residence that place where they should first be attacked by the aborigines of the country. On encamping for the night, a swarm of mice appeared and gnawed the leathern thongs of their armor, and accordingly they made that spot their home and erected a temple to Apollo Smintheus, this title being derived from the word meaning 'a rat' in the Aeolic dialect.

In ancient Troas mice were objects of worship; and the Greek writer, Heraclides Ponticus, said that they were held especially sacred at Chrysa, a town famous for its temple of Apollo. At Hamaxitus, too, mice were fed at the public expense.

Herodotus relates, on the authority of certain priests, that when in the year 699 BC Egypt was invaded by an Assyrian army under Sennacherib, it was revealed in a vision to the Egyptian king, Sethon, that he should receive assistance from the gods. And on the eve of an expected battle the camp of the Assyrians was attacked by a legion of field mice, who destroyed their quivers and bows, so that, being without serviceable weapons, the invaders fled in dismay on the ensuing morning. And in memory of this fabulous event a stone statue of King Sethon, bearing a mouse in his hand, was erected in the temple of Vulcan at Memphis, with this inscription: 'Whoever looks on me, let him revere the gods.'

Cicero, in his treatise on Divination, while commenting on the absurdity of the prevalent belief in prodigies, remarked that, if reliance were to be placed in omens of this kind, he ought naturally to tremble for the safety of the Commonwealth, because mice had recently nibbled a copy of Plato's *Republic* in his library.

Pliny wrote that rats foretold the Marsian war, 89 BC, by destroying silver shields and bucklers at Lavinium, an ancient city near Rome; and that they also prognosticated the death of the Roman general, Carbo, by eating his hose-garters and shoestrings at Clusium, the modern Chiusi, in Etruria. The same writer, in the eighth book of his *Natural History*, devotes a short chapter to an enumeration of instances, fabulous or historical, in which the inhabitants of several cities of the Roman Empire were driven from their homes by noxious animals, reptiles, and insects. He states, on the authority of the Greek moralist Theophrastus, that the natives of the island of Gyaros, one of the Cyclades, were forced to abandon their homes owing to the ravages of rats and mice, which devoured everything they could find, even including iron substances.

When the Philistines took the ark of the Lord from the camp of the Israelites, a plague of mice was sent to devastate their lands; whereupon the Philistines returned the ark, together with a trespass offering, which included five golden mice, as an atonement for their sacrilegious act.

In mediaeval legendary lore rats figure not unfrequently as avengers. The Polish king, Popiel II, who ascended the throne in the year 820, rendered himself obnoxious to his subjects by his immorality and tyranny, and, according to tradition, Heaven sent against him a multitude of rats, which pursued him constantly. The king and his family sought refuge in a castle situated on an island in the middle of Lake Goplo, on the Prussian frontier. But the rats finally invaded this stronghold and devoured the king and all belonging to him.

---

Again, in the year 970, so runs the legend, Hatto II, Archbishop of Mayence, who had made himself hateful to his people on account of his avarice and cruelty during a season of famine, was informed by one of his servants that a vast multitude of rats were advancing along the roads leading to the palace. The bishop betook himself at once to a tower in the middle of the Rhine, near Bingen, still known as the 'Mouse Tower', where he sought safety from his pursuers. But the rats swam out to the tower, gnawed through its walls, and devoured him. We read also in *A Chronicle of the Kings of England* that, in the reign of William the Conqueror, a great lord was attacked by mice at a banquet, and 'though he were removed from land to sea and from sea to land again', the mice pursued him to his death.

---

In Mexico rats were anciently the objects of superstitious regard, for they were credited with possessing a keen insight into the characters of all members of a household, and were wont publicly to announce flagrant breaches of morality on the part of such members by gnawing various articles of domestic furniture, such as mats and baskets. It does not appear, however, that the rodents were sagacious enough to indicate the individual whose conduct had aroused their displeasure.

The Mexicans had also a superstition that whoever partook of food which had been gnawed by rats would be falsely accused of some wrong-doing.

Rats and mice were not, however, the only agents employed as avengers. In the year 350, during a long siege of the Roman stronghold, Nisibis, in Mesopotamia, by the Persian king Sapor II, the inhabitants besought their bishop, St James, to utter a malediction against the enemy. Accordingly the prelate, standing on one of the wall towers, prayed God that a host of flies might be sent to attack the Persians, and tradition has it that the prayer was answered at once. A multitude of the insects descended upon the besiegers, their horses, and elephants; and men and animals, thus goaded to frenzy, were compelled to retreat, and so the siege was raised. The Philistines of old worshiped a special deity, Beelzebub, to whom they attributed the power of destroying flies. This same region is still infested with insect plagues; but the modern traveler, who has no faith in Beelzebub, is more likely to employ fly-traps and energetic practical measures.

Such are a few instances of the supernatural employment of vermin and insects as instruments of vengeance; and we need hardly wonder that, conversely, people in olden times should avail themselves of supernatural methods in order to protect themselves or their property from the ravages of these noxious creatures.

# SPIRITS ASSUME THE FORMS OF BLACK ANIMALS

The belief in the demoniacal possession of animals was prevalent in Europe for several centuries, and in order to drive away the evil spirits it was customary to employ various exorcisms and incantations, which were supposed to be infallible after approval by ecclesiastical authority.

---

Reginald Scot, in his *Discovery of Witchcraft*, says that, according to the testimony of reliable authors, spirits were wont to take the forms of animals, and especially of horses, dogs, swine, goats, and hares. They also appeared in the guise of crows and owls, but took the most delight in the likenesses of snakes and dragons. Bewitched animals were usually of a black color. A black cat is the traditional companion or familiar of witches the world over, and the black dog is also associated with sorcery in the folklore of some lands.

---

Among the Slavs the black demon Cernabog has this form, and the black hen is a common devil-symbol in mediaeval witch-lore. The gypsies believe, moreover, that black horses are gifted with a supernatural sight, which enables them to see beings invisible to the eye of man. Black animals figure prominently in many legends of the dark ages. Thus the Devil, in the form of a black horse, disturbed a congregation which had gathered to listen to a sermon delivered by St Peter of Verona in the thirteenth century, but was put to flight by the sign of the cross. Among birds the crow is considered an ominous creature in some countries, and in northeast Scotland is always associated with the 'black airt'. The raven, too, is traditionally portentous, and is sometimes called the Devil's bird; its plumage is said to have been changed from white to black on account of its disobedience. In Swedish legend the magpie shares the evil reputation of the raven and crow, and is characterized as 'a mystic bird, a downright witches' bird, belonging to the Devil and the other powers of the night'.

---

The Kirghis, a nomadic people of Turkestan, are very superstitious in regard to the magpie, and note with care the direction whence the sound of its cry is heard. If from the north, it portends evil; from the south, a remarkable occurrence; from the east, it denotes the coming of guests; and from the west, a journey.

---

The Rev. Alexander Stewart, in his *Nether Lochaber*, deprecates as unreasonable the universal distrust of the magpie. It seems probably that this is due less to its color than to certain other characteristics; for the magpie is a confirmed mimic and kleptomaniac, and of exceeding slyness withal.

---

Apropos of crows as foreboders, whether of good or evil, an amusing story is told of a man who wished to test for himself the truth or falsity of a popular belief that seeing a couple of crows in the early morning is a sign of good luck. He therefore directed his servant to awaken him at daybreak whenever two crows were to be seen. Accordingly one morning the servant called him, but in the meantime one of the birds had flown away. Thereupon the master became angry and gave his servant a sound beating, upbraiding him with having delayed until but one crow remained. The servant, however, nothing daunted, replied: 'Lo, sir, have you not seen the luck which is come to me from seeing two crows?'

Superstition has been defined as 'a belief not in accordance with the facts', but this is manifestly incorrect. An ignorant person, who thinks that black cats are more evil-minded than white ones, thereby cherishes a mistaken idea, but is not necessarily superstitious. If, however, he believes that a black cat or any other animal is endowed with a supernatural faculty of exerting evil influences over human beings, then he is not only ignorant, but also superstitious.

## EXORCISM AND CONJURATION OF VERMIN

The Grecian husbandmen were accustomed to drive away mice by writing them a message on a piece of paper and sticking it on a stone in the infested field. A specimen of such a message, beginning with an adjuration and concluding with a threat, is to be found in the *Geoponica*, a Grecian agricultural treatise.

In the endeavor to justify the employment of radical measures against vermin, some curious questions of casuistry were involved. Rats and mice being God's creatures, one ought not to take their lives. But it was considered entirely proper to drive them off one's own domain, while recommending as preferable the well-stocked cellar of a neighbor. Formulae of exorcism, or sentences containing warnings to depart, were written on scraps of paper, which were then well greased and rolled into little balls, or wrapped about poisoned edibles, and placed in the rat-holes.

---

Conjurations of vermin were usually in the name of St Gertrude, the first abbess of Nivelle in Belgium, and also the patron saint of travelers and cats, and protectress against the ravages of the smaller rodents.

---

The Spanish ecclesiastic, Martin Azpilcueta, surnamed Navarre, stated that when rats were exorcised, it was customary to banish them formally from the territory of Spain; and the creatures would then proceed to the seashore and swim to some remote island, where they made their home.

---

The public records of Hameln, in the kingdom of Hannover, state that in the year 1284 a stranger, in gay and fantastic attire, visited the town and proclaimed himself a professional rat-catcher, offering for a consideration to rid the place of the vermin which infested it. The townsfolk having agreed to his proposal, the stranger began to play a tune upon his pipe, whereupon the rats emerged in swarms from their hiding-places and followed him to the river Weser, where they were all drowned. The people of Hameln now repented of their bargain and refused to pay the full amount agreed upon, for the alleged reason that the rats had been driven away by the aid of sorcery. In revenge for this, the piper played the same tune on the next day, and immediately all the children of the town followed him to a cavern in the side of a neighboring hill, called the Koppenberg. The piper and the children entered the cavern, which closed after them; and in remembrance of this tragic event several memorials are to be seen in Hameln. Indeed, some writers maintain that the legend has an historical foundation, and such appears to have been the opinion of the townspeople, inasmuch as for years afterwards public and legal documents were dated from the mournful occurrence.

⁖·⁖

An old tradition says that mice originally fell upon the earth from the clouds during a thunderstorm, and hence these animals are emblematic of storms; they are also mystical creatures, and have a relationship with Donar, Wodan, and Frigg. In Bavaria profanity is thought to increase the number of mice in a dwelling, and their appearance in the fields in large numbers indicates war, pestilence, or famine. Bohemian peasants are wont to make a certain provision for these elfish rodents; on Christmas Eve and on the first holiday of the year, whatever food remains from the midday meal is thrown upon the barn floor, and the following sentence is repeated: mice, eat these remnants and leave the grain in peace! On Christmas Eve, also, peas are placed in heaps, shaped like a cross, in the four corners of a mouse-in-fested room, lest the vermin get the upper hand and the premises be overrun. In eastern Prussia, when the harvest is gathered, the last sheaf of corn is left standing in the field, while the peasants surround it and sing a hymn as an incantation against future devastation of their lands by rats or mice. Or, when the corn is harvested, three inverted sheaves are fixed upon the barn floor for a like purpose.

<hr />

According to a Bohemian legend, the mouse was originally a creation of the Devil, at the time when Noah entered the Ark, attended by the members of his family and followed by a numerous retinue of animals. The Devil, so runs the tale, hated the patriarch for his piety, and with evil intent created the mouse, whom he sent to gnaw a hole in the side of the Ark, through which the water might enter. But God then created the cat, who pursued and devoured the mouse, thus frustrating the design of the Evil One.

<hr />

At the siege of Angers, the ancient capital of Anjou, in the year 845, during the reign of King Charles the Bald, the French were much annoyed by swarms of grasshoppers of unusual size. They were duly exorcised according to the custom of the times, and having been put to flight, are reported to have precipitated themselves into a river.

<hr />

The French writer, St Foix, in his *Essais historiques sur Paris*, has recorded that in the year 1120, the Bishop of Laon, in the Department of Aisne, pronounced an injunction against field mice, on account of their ravages; and St Bernard, a contemporary of that prelate, while preaching at Foigny in the same diocese, in order to relieve his congregation of the annoyance caused by a multitude of flies, repeated a formula of excommunication against them, whereat, according to monkish records, the flies fell dead in heaps and were gathered up with shovels. The early Anglo-Saxons not only made use of amulets of wood or other material, on which were engraven Runic characters, to secure protection from elves and demons, but they carried about with them the herb called periwinkle, of the botanical genus Vinca, as a charm against snakes and wild animals.

---

## CHARMS AGAINST ANIMALS

As illustrative of the superstitious use of charms and exorcisms against animals and reptiles in different epochs and countries, we have examples from many and varied sources.

---

The Egyptians used, as charms against venomous serpents, various magic formulae inscribed upon strips of papyrus, which were rolled up and worn as talismans. A specimen of such a one is to be seen among the Egyptian manuscripts in the Louvre collection. The following is a translation of a portion of one of these incantations, which invokes the aid of a god to protect the bearer against wild animals and reptiles:

'Come to me, O Lord of Gods, drive far from me the lions coming from the earth, the crocodiles issuing from the river, the mouth of all biting reptiles coming out of their holes.'

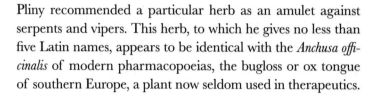

Pliny recommended a particular herb as an amulet against serpents and vipers. This herb, to which he gives no less than five Latin names, appears to be identical with the *Anchusa officinalis* of modern pharmacopoeias, the bugloss or ox tongue of southern Europe, a plant now seldom used in therapeutics.

The Grecians also were doubtless addicted to the superstitious use of charms against animals, although there is good authority for the statement that the citizens of ancient Athens did not hesitate on occasion to accelerate the 'flight of ominous creatures, as cats and the like' by throwing stones or other handy missiles at them in the night, a method wholly mundane and natural. And in this connection we may quote the opinion of the Rev. Father Pierre Le Brun, in his *Histoire critique des pratiques superstitieuses*. The learned writer remarks that, if it were desired to drive a strange dog out of one's room, it would be quite unsuitable to begin with prayer and the use of holy water. One should rather first open the door and take hold of a stick, or throw some food outside; and if these and other practical measures fail, then recourse may be had to supernatural expedients, provided these have ecclesiastical sanction.

In a treatise against superstition by a French savant, Martin of Aries, published in 1650, it was stated that the friars of the monastery of Ardennes were wont to boast that no rats could thrive in their neighborhood, and that this fact was due to the merits of St Ulric, Bishop of Augsburg, some of whose relics were deposited in their church. In this monastery also it had been formerly customary to scatter crumbs of bread which had been blessed, in places infested by vermin, and the monks believed that this procedure either caused the death of the animals or frightened them away.

<hr />

Thuringian houses are sometimes cleared of rats in the following manner: before sunrise on Good Friday morning, the master of the house, barefooted and in his shirt sleeves, goes through every room blowing on a tiny whistle made out of the thigh bone of a rat's hind leg. Another curious method of expelling vermin from a dwelling is in vogue in some portions of the Austrian Empire. Before the dawn of a principal feast day, one must take an old shoe which has not been recently cleaned, and lay it on the ground at a place where two roads cross. No word must meanwhile be spoken aloud, but a Paternoster is to be silently repeated. The direction in which the shoe points indicates the course to be taken by the rats in their flight. In the village of Bechlin, a few miles north of Prague, troublesome mice are thus dealt with: very early on an Easter Sunday morning, before the bells have rung for the first Mass, the peasant matron collects and fastens together all the house keys. Then she waits until the first stroke of the bell for High Mass at noon, whereupon she proceeds to the cellar, meanwhile jingling the keys vigorously so long as the church bells ring; when they cease she retraces her steps, still rattling the keys; and these measures are believed to permanently frighten away the mice.

---

Towards the middle of the seventeenth century a great army of locusts invaded the fields in the neighborhood of the town of Mixco, in Guatemala. So numerous were they as for a time to obscure the light of the sun, and to break the branches of the trees whereon they clung; and they speedily devoured the corn and other crops. Moreover, they covered the highways and startled the traveling mules by their fluttering movements. By order of the magistrates, the people of the country assembled in the fields with trumpets and other instruments in order to scare away the unwelcome visitors. Idols were brought out, especially pictures of the Virgin and of St Nicholas Tolentine. From the country regions near and far came the Spanish farmers to the town of Mixco, with propitiatory offerings for the saint, and all brought with them loaves of bread to be blessed. These loaves they carried back to their farms, and either threw into their cornfields or buried beneath their hedges, hoping by this method to protect their crops from the locusts.

---

The mountain ash, or rowan tree (the Scotch *rountree*), is thought to have derived its name from the Latin word *runa*, an incantation, because of its employment in magical arts. Woe to the witch who is touched by a branch of this tree in the hand of a christened man!

Much has been written concerning the folklore of the mountain ash, and it is indeed a powerful rival of the horseshoe in its talismanic virtues, though not as a luck-bringer.

But for the protection of cattle from the incursions of witches, not even the horseshoe may assume to usurp the rowan's prestige. Branches of this favorite tree, when hung over the stalls of cows or wreathed about their horns, are potent to avert the evil glances or contact, whether of witches or malicious fairies. And their efficacy is enhanced if the farmer is careful to repeat at regular intervals the following fervent petition: 'From Witches and Wizards, and long-tailed Buzzards, and creeping things that run in hedge bottoms, good Lord, deliver us!'

Jamieson, in his *Scottish Dictionary*, remarks that this practice of twining the rowan about the horns of cows bears a certain resemblance to an ancient custom of the Romans in their Palilla, or feast celebrated at the end of April, whose object was the preservation of the flocks. He says: 'The Shepherd, in order to purify his sheep, was in the dusk of the evening to bedew the ground around them with a wet branch, then to adorn the fold with leaves and green branches and to cover the door with garlands.'

In China it is customary for the Taouist priests to perform certain magical rites on the completion of a new pigsty, and before the admission of the animals to their new quarters. An altar is erected in honor of the Chu-Lan-Too-Tee, or genii of pigsties, and the walls of the compartments of the sty are adorned with strips of red paper, upon which are Chinese characters, signifying, 'Let the enemies of horses, cows, sheep, fowls, dogs, and pigs be appeased.'

# WORDS USED AS CHARMS

The English word 'charm' is derived from the Latin *carmen*, a verse; and the magical potency of a sentence used as a charm was believed to rest in the words themselves, and not in the person who uttered them. In the opinion of the cabalistic magicians of the Middle Ages, the power of a charm of words depended upon its being unintelligible.

The Latin poet, Varius, wrote in the first century BC. that old women, by the sole use of words as charms, were able not only to restrain and subjugate wild animals and serpents, but also to drive away noxious creatures and vermin. Few early writers allude to this practice, which appears, however, to have been much in vogue in different countries towards the close of the mediaeval period.

The Swiss theologian Felix Hammerlein wrote of a peasant living near Zurich who was able, by repeating a magic formula, to rid infested premises of adders, vipers, lizards, and other reptiles; and in some parts of Normandy it was a custom formerly to place small rolls of hay under the fruit trees. The hay was then set on fire by means of torches carried by young children, who repeated meanwhile: 'Mice, caterpillars, and moles, get out of my field; I will burn your beard and your bones; trees and shrubs, give me three bushels of apples.' Hampson remarks that this incantation somewhat resembles one employed by the ancient Grecians against beetles, whom they held responsible for the destruction of their corn. These magical lines are thus translated: 'Fly, beetles, the ravenous wolf pursues you.'

---

It was currently reported among the ancients that the famous philosopher, Pythagoras, not only possessed the faculty of predicting storms and earthquakes, but that he had by a magical word been enabled to tame a Daunian bear, and had also prevented an ox from eating beans by whispering in his ear.

---

Antoine Mizauld, the French physician and astrologer, affirmed that, according to Ptolemy, in order to drive away serpents, one should prepare a talisman by engraving the figure of two serpents upon a square piece of copper and pronouncing a charm of words as follows: 'With this image I forbid serpents to harm anyone, and command them to leave the place where it shall be buried.' In like manner, says the same authority, to expel rats and mice, one has only to represent an image of one of these creatures upon a piece of tin or copper, and at the proper time, as determined by astrology, command them to depart.

───⚜··⚜───

In order to expel snakes, insects, and vermin from their dwellings, the Bulgarian women of Turkey, on the last day of February, endeavor to frighten the creatures by beating copper vessels all over the house, while shouting, 'Out with you, snakes, scorpions, flies, bugs, and fleas!' One of the vessels is then taken into the courtyard, the pests being expected to follow it.

───⚜··⚜───

And in Serfo, an island of the Grecian archipelago, at the commencement of the vintage a bunch of grapes is thrown into each house to expel the vermin, while this formula is repeated: 'The black grape will sicken you; the black grape will poison you! Out with you, rats and fleas!'

───⚜··⚜───

In Albania, when locusts or cockchafers devastate the fields, a number of women, having caught some of the insects, form a mock funeral procession, and proceed to drown them in some convenient stream. And while on their way thither they chant in turn the following dirge, which all repeat in chorus: 'O locusts, O cockchafers, parents kind, Orphaned you have left us all behind.' And this proceeding is thought to be destructive to the whole swarm of insects.

───⚜··⚜───

The following charm against foxes was formerly used in France, and was to be repeated thrice a week: 'Foxes, both male and female, I conjure you in the name of the Holy Trinity, that ye neither touch nor carry off any of my fowls, whether roosters, hens or chickens; nor eat their nests, nor suck their blood, nor break their eggs, nor do them any harm whatever.'

---

The Roman Catholic Church formerly sanctioned the use of certain sentences as charms against vipers, and the following may serve as a specimen:

> I conjure thee, O serpent, in this hour, by the five holy wounds of Our Lord, that thou remove not out of this place, as certainly as God was born of a pure Virgine. Otherwise, I conjure thee, serpent, by Our Lady St Mary, that thou obey me, as wax obeyeth the fire, and as fire obeyeth water, that thou neither hurt me nor any other Christian, as certainly as God was born of an immaculate Virgine, in which respect I take thee up. *In Nomine Patris et Filii et Spiritus Sancti…* Otherwise, O vermine, thou must come as God came unto the Jews.

---

When a Turk chances to encounter a serpent, he is wont to invoke the aid of Chah-Miran, the serpent king, and in the name of this deity he bids the reptile depart. Now Chah-Miran has long been dead, but the astute Turk reasons that serpents are not aware of this fact, for, if they were, the human race would be helpless against their attacks.

As preservatives from the stings of insects, and to prevent the croaking of frogs, the Muslims use scraps of paper containing magical formulae, or sentences from the Koran engraved on stones or pieces of metal; and a method formerly in vogue in France, to protect pigeons from the incursions of scorpions, consisted in writing the word 'Adam' on each of the four walls of the pigeon house.

The natives of Mirzapur, in cases of scorpion bite, recite a charm meaning as follows: 'Black scorpion of the limestone, green thy tail and black thy mouth, God orders thee to go home. Come out, scorpion, at the spell. Come out, come out!'

The following charm against insects is in vogue in Lesbos: in the evening a black-handled knife is stuck in some spot where the insects congregate, and certain Greek verses are repeated, of which the following is a translation:

*I got three naughty bairns together,*
*One a wasp, one caterpillar,*
*And a swarming ant the other.*
*Whate'er ye eat, whate'er ye drink,*
*Hence, hence avaunt.*

*To the hills and mountains flee,*
*And unto each fruitless tree.*

The knife is to remain in the same spot until the next morning, and is then to be removed. This completes the charm, and the insects are expected to depart at once.

In Great Britain there formerly prevailed a belief that rats could be rhymed to death by anathematizing them in metrical verse, a practice mentioned by Shakespeare and contemporary poets, and which is even today not wholly obsolete.

In southern Germany, during the campaigns of Napoleon I, mice with inked feet were placed upon the map of Europe, and their tracks were held to foretell the routes by which the French soldiers would advance.

The Hindus consider the rat to be a sacred animal, and among the lower classes of the natives of western India it is thought unlucky to call a rat by his own name, so they speak of him as the 'rat uncle'.

# SUPERSTITIOUS
## DEALINGS WITH WILD ANIMALS

In encountering a wild animal, the ancients deemed it a matter of great importance that a man should see the beast before the latter was aware of a human presence. If a wolf, for example, first perceived the man, the brute was master of the situation, and the man was bereft alike of speech and strength; whereas the wolf, if first seen by the man, became an easy prey. The side from which a wild beast approached was also of moment. Thus the *Geoponica* warned its readers not to allow a hyena to approach from the right side, lest one be rendered motionless by the fascination of its presence; but if it appeared on the left side, the animal might be attacked with confidence.

---

Various wonderful tales are current among the natives of Senegambia, and other districts of western Africa, regarding the lion. This noble animal, it is said, forbears to attack a man who salutes him with a respectful gesture, and the same gallant instinct restrains the beast from harming a woman. In most lion-haunted regions, however, the natives do not have such implicit confidence in the courtesy and forbearance of wild animals, but trust rather to the efficacy of various amulets. The Kaffirs of south eastern Africa, for example, on encountering a lion or leopard in the forest, proceed at once to nibble a so-called lion-charm, which is merely a small bit of wood or root. And if the animal moves away without molesting him, the Kaffir attributes his security to the magic power of the charm, not realizing that his escape is due to the natural dread of man which is characteristic of animals generally.

So, too, the priests of Mexico were accustomed to rub their bodies with a certain ointment which they believed to be an efficient protection against wild beasts, its pungent odor acting as a charm, so that they were enabled to wander unmolested amid the wildest solitudes. The skilled hunter, however, confident in his own prowess, depends neither upon the alleged gallantry of lions nor the potency of amulets, but rather on his trusty rifle.

The belief in charms against noxious animals is widespread; for not alone in African jungles does this form of superstition prevail: it is found among civilized people as well, and more particularly in southern lands; indeed, wherever venomous creatures abound. In a collection of amulets belonging to Professor Joseph Belucci, of Perugia, Italy, which was exhibited at the Paris Exposition 1891, were a number of perforated stones and other objects used by Italians as charms to protect the bearer against the bite of serpents and reptiles.

## LEGAL PROSECUTION OF ANIMALS

Legal proceedings were formerly instituted against vermin, who were thus treated as if they were human beings endowed with consciences and responsible for their actions. Prosecutions of animals were common in France and Switzerland, with a view to protect communities from their depredations. Thus rats and mice, and also bulls, oxen, cows, and mares; sheep, goats, pigs, and dogs; moles, leeches, caterpillars, and various reptiles, were liable to punishment by legal process.

---

The Roman Catholic Church claimed full power to anathematize all animate and inanimate things, founding its authority on the Scriptural precedents of the malediction pronounced on the serpent in the Garden of Eden, and the cursing of the barren fig tree by our Lord. The belief in the moral responsibility of animals was also thought to be warranted by the old Mosaic law as declared in Genesis ix. 5: 'And surely your blood of your lives will I require; at the hand of every beast will I require it, and at the hand of man.'

---

Also in Exodus 11: 28: 'If an ox gore a man or a woman, that they die: then the ox shall be surely stoned, and his flesh shall not be eaten; but the owner of the ox shall be quit.'

---

In the Code of the Spartan lawgiver, Lycurgus, and in that of the Athenian legislator, Draco, provision was made for the formal trial of animals for misdemeanors. A vestige of the unreasonable belief that brutes and even inanimate objects were accountable for their actions is to be found in that now obsolete term of English law, *deodand*, meaning, according to Blackstone, 'a personal chattel which was the immediate cause of the death of a rational creature, and for that reason given to God; that is, forfeited to the Crown to be applied to pious uses.' The *deodand* was of Grecian ancestry, as appears from the ceremonies connected with the offering of a sacrifice by the Athenians. When the animal or victim had been dispatched by an axe in the hands of the officiating priest, the latter immediately fled, and to evade arrest he threw away the axe. This instrument was then seized by his pursuers, and an action entered against it. The advocate for the axe pleaded that it was less guilty than the grinder who sharpened it; the grinder laid the blame on the grindstone which he had used; and thus the whole process became a farce and a mockery of justice.

---

We learn from the writings of the Benedictine monk, Leonard Vair, that in certain districts of Spain, in the fifteenth century, when the inhabitants wished to drive away grasshoppers or noxious vermin, they chose a conjurer as judge and appointed counsel for the defendants, with a prosecuting attorney, who demanded justice in behalf of the aggrieved community. The mischief makers were finally declared guilty, and either duly anathematized or formally excommunicated, the technical distinction between the two sentences being doubtless to them a matter of profound indifference. At this period, also, prosecutions of pigs or sows guilty of devouring young infants were not uncommon.

---

Barthelemy Chassaneux, a famous French advocate of the sixteenth century, first won distinction by the originality of his pleas in defense of some rats in a notable trial at Autun. He represented to the judge that his clients found it extremely difficult to obey the summons issued to them by the court, owing to their being obliged to traverse a region abounding in cats, who were, moreover, especially alert on account of the notoriety of the legal proceedings.

———————❧•❧———————

Chassaneux wrote that the people of Autun had long agitated the question how best to rid the province of Burgundy of locusts, and he expressed the belief that a sure method of accomplishing so desirable a result was by the scrupulous payment of all tithes and ecclesiastical dues, and by causing a woman to walk barefoot round the infested fields.

———————❧•❧———————

After the seventeenth century, prosecutions of animals and the use of incantations for their expulsion became less common. The Ritual of Seez in 1743 forbade such practices without the special permission of the church, but the same volume contains a formula for driving away grasshoppers, maybugs, and other insects. Mr C.G. Leland states, in his *Gypsy Sorcery*, that exorcism has been vigorously applied in the United States, not only against the Colorado beetle and army worm, but also for the suppression of blizzards and the grape disease. It has not had much success hitherto, probably owing, as he naively remarks, to the uncongenial climate.

———————❧•❧———————

# THE LUCK OF
# ODD NUMBERS

## EARLY SIGNIFICANCE
## OF NUMBERS

In the 'Cabala', or ancient mystic philosophy of the Jews, much importance is attributed to the combination of certain numbers, letters, and words. According to one tradition, the earliest Cabala was given by the angel Raziel to Adam, and orally transmitted through generations until the time of Solomon, by whom it was first embodied in written form. Another report alleges that the cabalistic secrets of nature were received from God by Moses in the Mount, and afterwards taught to Joshua, who communicated them to the seventy elders, and they have since been treasured by the initiated among the Jews.

---

According to the doctrine of the Pythagoreans, the unit or *monad* was regarded as the father of Numbers, while the *duad*, or two, was its mother; and thus is explained one source of the general predilection for odd numbers, the father being esteemed worthy of greater honor than the mother, and the odd numbers being masculine, while the even numbers were feminine. Moreover, the unit, being the origin of all numbers, represented Divinity, as God was the creator and originator of all things. It was also the symbol of Harmony and Order, whereas the *duad* signified Confusion and Disorder, and represented the Devil.

---

Plutarch remarks in his 'Roman Questions' that the beginning of number, or unity, is a divine thing; whereas the first of the even numbers, Deuz or Deuce, is directly opposite in character. As for the even number, said this writer, it is defective, imperfect, and indefinite; whereas the uneven or odd number is finite, complete, and absolute.

---

The belief in the lucky significance of odd numbers is of great antiquity, and reference to it is made by Virgil in the eighth Eclogue, and by Pliny, who comments on its prevalence in his time, but offers no explanation therefore. The Roman king, Numa Pompilius, is said to have added days to certain months in order to make an odd number.

---

It is related, moreover, that the Emperor Julius Caesar, having once been thrown out of his chariot through some mishap, refused thereafter to set out upon a drive or journey until he had thrice repeated a magic formula; and this practice appears to have been commonly in vogue in those days.

---

The persistency of a traditional belief is exemplified by the modern association of luck with uneven numbers; and probably the Goddess Fortune herself preferred a three-legged stool. However this may be, it is evident that the legions of her worshipers today are firmly convinced of the mystic charm inherent in triplets. The Chinese pagodas, or sacred towers, built by devout persons with the object of improving the luck of a neighborhood, have always an odd number of stories, being from three to thirteen floors high. In Siam, also, this superstition holds universal sway, and its influence in the construction of buildings is especially noticeable; for the Siamese religiously adhere to odd numbers in architecture, and every house must have an uneven number of rooms, windows, and doors; each staircase must have an uneven number of steps.

———— ❧ ‧ ❧ ————

In the early literature and mythology of the Northern nations much importance was attached to the numbers three and nine, which were held especially sacred and dear to the gods. This fact is shown in their religious ceremonies, and more particularly in their sacrifices, which occurred every ninth month. Each sacrifice, moreover, lasted nine days, and each day nine victims, whether men or animals, were offered up.

———— ❧ ‧ ❧ ————

## THE NUMBER THREE

Three, as emblematic of the Trinity, has always been considered a sacred number, and long before the Christian era God was worshiped as a triple Deity. This is true not only of the Assyrians, Phoenicians, Greeks, and Romans, but also of the ancient Scandinavians, the Druids, the inhabitants of Mexico and Peru, as well as the Chinese and Japanese.

So from earliest times the Hindus have worshiped their triad of Brahma, Vishnu and Siva. In Holy Writ we find three sister virtues. Faith, Hope, and Charity; and in classic mythology are trios of Graces, Fates, and Furies, the three-forked lightning of Jupiter, the three-headed dog, Cerberus, and the trident of Neptune. The tripod was anciently a symbol of prophecy and of divine authority, and the triangle was originally the pagan emblem of a holy triad.

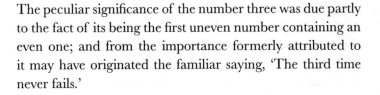

The peculiar significance of the number three was due partly to the fact of its being the first uneven number containing an even one; and from the importance formerly attributed to it may have originated the familiar saying, 'The third time never fails.'

In the several codes of ancient Welsh laws are numerous so-called triads, of which the following are curious examples:

> Three things which a villain is not at liberty
> to sell without permission of his lord; a horse,
> swine, and honey. Three things not to be paid
> for though lost in a lodging-house; a knife, a
> sword, and trousers. There are three animals

whose tails, eyes, and lives are of the same worth; a calf, a filly for common worth, and a cat, excepting the cat that shall watch the king's barn.

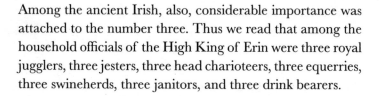

Among the ancient Irish, also, considerable importance was attached to the number three. Thus we read that among the household officials of the High King of Erin were three royal jugglers, three jesters, three head charioteers, three equerries, three swineherds, three janitors, and three drink bearers.

Multiples of the mystic number three were much employed by witches in their incantations, and they are even now favorites with the Chinese, who have a saying that one produced two and two produced three, while three produced all things. This partiality is illustrated in the dimensions of the Temple of Heaven in Peking, where three and nine constantly recur.

In a book entitled *Varieties*, by David Person, being 'a surveigh of rare and excellent matters, necessary and delectable for all sorts of persons', the author comments at some length on the significance of certain triads. Among others he mentions three things incident to man – to fall into sin, which is human; to rise out of it again, which is angelical; and to lie in sin, which is diabolical. Again, three powerful enemies, the world, the flesh, and the Devil, which constantly assail man, should be opposed by three efficient weapons, fasting, prayer, and almsgiving. Thomas Vaughan, in his *Anthroposophia Theomagica*, has much to say concerning the virtues of numbers. 'Every compound whatsoever,' he says, 'is three in one and one in three.' In speaking of a natural triplicity, however, he does not wish to be understood as referring to 'kitchen-stuff, those three pet principles, water, oil, and the earth, but to celestial hidden natures, known only to absolute magicians.'

------------

In Northumberland smooth holly leaves, gathered late on a Friday, are collected in a three-cornered handkerchief and carried home. Then nine of the leaves are tied into a handkerchief with nine knots, and placed under the would-be diviner's pillow, and, as a result, interesting revelations from dreamland are confidently anticipated. In another magical ceremony, a maiden before retiring sets three pails of water on the floor of her bedroom, and pins three holly leaves on her left breast. She will then, conformably to the popular belief, be awakened from her first nap by three loud yells, followed by three horse-laughs, whereupon the form of her future husband will be revealed to her.

------------

The supposed efficacy of these rites doubtless depends chiefly upon the use of the magical holly, but the repetition of odd numbers is also characteristic of charms, incantations, and mystic procedures in all ages and throughout the world.

------------

# THE NUMBER SEVEN

The number seven has ever been regarded as having a peculiar mystic significance, and its manifold virtues have been the theme of elaborate monographs. Alike in Holy Writ and among the earliest historic peoples, in classic antiquity and in the mythologies of many nations, this number has been most prominent, and to this fact may reasonably be attributed a portion of the luck associated with odd numbers in general. A complete enumeration of familiar examples of the use of this favorite number, although germane to our subject, would be beyond the scope of this sketch, but a few instances may be appropriately given.

---

The origin of the respect accorded this number by the nations of antiquity was probably astronomical, or more properly astrological, and arose from their observation of the seven great planets and of the lunar phases, changing every seventh day. 'Saturn is first, next Jove, Mars third in place; The Sun in midst, fifth Venus runs her race, Mercury sixth, Moon lowest and last in band. The Planets in this rank and manner stand.'

---

It was a saying of Hippocrates that the number seven, by reason of its mystic virtues, tended to the accomplishment of all things, and was the dispenser of life and the fountain of all its changes; for as the moon changes its phases every seven days, so this number influences all sublunary beings.

The phrase 'to be in the seventh heaven' was derived from the seven planets, which were believed by the Babylonians to be carried around upon as many globes of crystal, the seventh being the highest. In the writings of the Cabalists of old are likewise portrayed seven heavens, one above another, and the seventh or highest was the abode of God and the higher angels. The ultimate source of the sanctity of the number seven has, however, been ascribed to the *septentriones*, the seven ploughing oxen, stars of the constellation of the Great Bear.

---

An ingenious but not especially plausible reason alleged for the popularity of this number is the fact of its being composed of *three*, the number of sides in a triangle, and *four*, the number of sides in a square, thus representing two of the simplest geometric figures.

Certain Biblical critics of a speculative turn of mind have concluded that its prominence as a symbol is due to the emblematic significance of its component parts, three and four; the former representing Divinity, and the latter Humanity: in other words, 'the union between God and man, as affected by the manifestations of the Divinity in creation and revelation.'

---

In some portions of a great work on magic, discovered by Mr A.H. Layard among fragments of clay tablets in the ruins of a palace in ancient Nineveh, are many incantations, formulae, and conjurations, in which the number seven occurs repeatedly.

---

As familiar instances of the prominence of this number in former times may be cited the seven wise men of Greece, the seven gates of Thebes, and the legend of the seven sleepers of Ephesus.

---

In ancient Ireland every well-to-do farmer had seven prime possessions – a house, a mill or a share in it, a kiln, barn, sheep-pen, calf-house, and pigsty.

---

The number seven appears more than 300 times in the Scriptures. God created the world in six days and rested on the seventh, and throughout the Old Testament, as well as in the Apocalypse, the constant recurrence of this sacred number is noteworthy. Thus we read of the seven fat and seven lean kine of Pharaoh's dream, and also, in the account of the Fall of Jericho (Joshua 4:4): 'And seven priests shall bear before the ark seven trumpets of rams' horns: and the seventh day ye shall compass the city seven times, and the priests shall blow with the trumpets.'

---

According to a popular mediaeval tradition, Adam and Eve remained but seven hours in Eden.

---

Seven archangels are mentioned in the Bible and in Jewish writings – *Michael*, who was the special guardian and protector of the Jews, and in whose honor the Festival of Michaelmas is celebrated on the twenty-ninth day of September by the Anglican and Roman Catholic churches; *Gabriel*, the messenger who appeared to the Virgin Mary and to Zacharias; *Raphael*, spoken of in the Book of Tobit as the companion and guardian of Tobias, and conqueror of the demon Asmodeus; *Uriel*, an angel mentioned in the Book of Esdras; *Chamuel*, who, according to Jewish tradition, wrestled with Jacob; *Jophiel*, who expelled Adam and Eve from Eden, and who was the guardian of the 'tree of the knowledge of good and evil'; and *Zadkiel*, the angel who is supposed to have stayed the hand of Abraham when the latter was about to sacrifice his son Isaac.

———— ⚜ ⚜ ————

Samson's strength resided in seven locks of his hair, representing the seven rays of Light, the source of Strength. And the shearing of these seven locks by Delilah, a woman of low character, has been described as a triumph of Evil in suppressing Light.

———— ⚜ ⚜ ————

According to Herodotus, the Arabs of the desert had a peculiar method of confirming a vow of friendship. Two men stood on either side of a third, who made incisions with a sharp stone on the palms of their hands, and, having dipped in the blood therefrom some portion of a garment of each, he proceeded to moisten with it seven stones lying on the ground.

---

The age of the world, in the opinion of learned men of former times, was properly divided into seven great epochs; namely, the first, from the creation of Adam to the Deluge; second, from the latter event to the time of Abraham; third, from Abraham to the Exodus of the children of Israel; fourth, from that time to the building of Solomon's Temple; fifth, from then to the Babylonish Captivity; sixth, the period between that and the coming of our Lord; and seventh, from the beginning of the Christian era to the end of the world.

---

According to astrologers, man's age was divided into seven parts, governed by seven planets. The first part Infancy, comprised four years, and was ruled by the Moon, a weak, moist, and changeable body. Next came Childhood, a period of ten years governed by Mercury, a planet indifferently good or bad, according to the character of the planets with whom he was associated. Following this came Youthhead, from fourteen to twenty-two, over which Venus presided. Next was Adolescence, lasting twenty years and ruled by the Sun, and in this age man attained his full strength and vigor. The fifth, from forty-two to fifty-six, was called Manhood, and was under the dominion of Mars, a bad star. At this time men began to wax angry, impatient, and avaricious, but were more temperate in their diet, and more discreet. The next period of twelve years was called Old Age, governed by Jupiter, a noble planet, whose influence rendered men religious, chaste, and just. The seventh was Decrepit Old Age, ruled by Saturn, and comprising the years from seventy-eight to ninety-eight.

In the Lambeth Palace Library there is a manuscript of the fifteenth century in which the seven canonical hours are compared with the seven periods of human life, as follows:

| | |
|---|---|
| Morning | Infancy. |
| Midmorrow | Childhood. |
| Undern | School Age. |
| Mid-day | Knightly Age. |
| Nones, or High Noon | the Kingly Age. |
| Midovernoon | Elderly Age. |
| Evenson | Declining Age. |

In the 'Secrets of Numbers' by William Ingpen the number seven is described as the most excellent of all for several notable and curious reasons, and prominent among these was the alleged fact that the Soul consists of seven parts, namely, Acuminie, Wit, Diligence, Counsel, Reason, Wisdom, and Experience.

## ODD NUMBERS
## IN WITCHCRAFT

Odd numbers are intimately associated with the black art, for witches' incantations are commonly repeated three or nine times. Who ever heard of a witch performing any of her mystic rites exactly four or six times? Apropos of this may be quoted the following story, taken from the advance sheets of a work entitled *Golspie*, edited by Edward W.B. Nicholson, Bodley's Librarian in the University of Oxford, England, and loaned by him to the writer. The book contains much interesting folklore of the extreme north of Scotland:

> A woman who lived near Golspie was always telling her neighbors that a woman whom they all believed to be a witch had cast an evil eye upon the cow and herself. 'Her milk and butter were spoiled,' she said; and she also told them that in a dream she saw the witch in the shape of a hare come into her milk-house and drink the milk. One day when she was in the wood for sticks, her neighbors went into her byre, and seeing a petticoat on a nail, cut a number of crosses on it and put it in the cow's stall. Then they tied nine rusty nails to a cord with nine knots on it. This cord they tied to the chain on the cow's neck, and then went away. Shortly after the woman came home, she went into the byre, and seeing the petticoat, nails, etc., ran out to her neighbors screaming, and calling to them to go and see what the witch had done on her. To make sure that it was the witch's work, she showed them the *unequal number* of nails and knots. Then she took everything that she thought the witch had handled, and made a fire of them, saying that she could no longer harm any person, because her power was destroyed by fire.

The employment of odd numbers in magical formulae is exemplified in the following recipe for a drink against all temptations of the Devil, used by the Saxons in England:

> Take betony, bishopwort, lupins, githrife, attor-lothe, wolfs-comb, yarrow; lay them under the altar, sing nine masses over them, scrape the worts into holy water, give the man to drink at night, fasting, a cup-full, and put the holy water into all the meat which the man taketh. Work thus a good salve against the temptations of the fiend.

———————— ❖⋅⋅❖ ————————

A Hindu woman, on returning with her young child from a strange village, is careful, before entering her own dwelling, to pass seven small stones seven times around the baby's head, and throw them away in different directions, in order thus to disperse any evil which may have been contracted during her trip.

And as a preliminary to other mystic procedures, in order to avert the Evil Eye, the Hindus wave around the patient's face seven pebbles taken from a spot where three roads meet, seven leaves of the date-palm, and seven bunches of leaves of the *bor* tree.

———————— ❖⋅⋅❖ ————————

Charms and formulas are commonly thrice repeated, probably in reference to the Holy Trinity.

> *Of all the numbers arithmeticall,*
> *The number three is heald for principall,*

*As well in naturall philosophy,*
*As supernaturall theologie.*

———————⚜••⚜———————

The Bavarian peasant, in passing through a haunted place, considers himself amply fortified against evil if he takes the precaution to carry three things; namely, (1) a new knife which has never cut anything, marked on the blade with three crosses; (2) a loaf of bread baked on Epiphany Eve; (3) a black cat.

———————⚜••⚜———————

## ODD NUMBERS
## IN FOLK MEDICINE

In a volume containing a great variety of ancient charms and magical cures, collected by Marcellus Empiricus, a Latin writer of the fourth century AD, in which volume various remedial measures are described with great minuteness, the even numbers seldom appear.

Thus, for the removal of a foreign substance from the eye, one should rub the affected organ with the five fingers of the hand of the same side, and repeat thrice a charm of words. Again, for the cure of a sty on the eyelid, take nine grains of barley and poke the sty with each one separately, meanwhile repeating a magic formula in Greek. Then throw away the nine and do the same with seven, throw away the seven and do the same with five, and so with three and one.

———————⚜••⚜———————

The early Saxon physicians in England seem also to have had faith in the peculiar virtues of the number nine, as is evident from many of their prescriptions, of which the following prefix to a lengthy Latin charm is a fair specimen:

> For flying venom and every venomous swelling,
> on a Friday churn butter which has been milked
> from a neat or hind all of one colour, and let
> it not be mingled with water. Sing over it nine
> times a litany and nine times the Paternoster,
> and nine times this incantation.

---

In an ancient English manuscript, frequent examples are given of the employment of odd numbers in therapeutics. Thus, for dropsical affections, a beverage containing alexander, betony, and fennel is to be drunk daily for seven days. 'To expel venom' centaury is to be taken for fifteen days, and a potion prepared from the seed of cress is extolled for its curative qualities if taken faithfully during three days.

---

Indeed, the odd numbers are prominent in the annals of folk medicine throughout Great Britain. The three chief duties of a physician were declared to be as follows: the restoration of health when lost, its amelioration when weak, and its preservation when recovered. So also three qualities were requisite in a surgeon; namely, an eagle's eye, a lion's heart, and a lady's hand, attributes equally essential to the skillful operator of the present day.

———— ❧ ❧ ————

The natives of the Hebrides inherit the old Scandinavian and Celtic partiality for certain odd numbers. Thus in Tiree a favorite cure for jaundice consists in wearing a shirt previously dipped in water taken from the tops of nine waves, and in which nine stones have been boiled. These same people formerly employed a peculiar method of treating sick cattle. The veterinary, holding in his hands a cup of cream and an oatcake, takes his seat upon the animal, and repeats a Celtic charm of words 'nine times nine times', taking 'a bit and a sip' before each repetition.

———— ❧ ❧ ————

In Cornwall, for the cure of inflammatory affections, the invocation of three angels is thrice repeated to each one of nine bramble leaves; and a popular remedy for whooping cough is to pass a child nine times under and over a three-year-old donkey.

———— ❧ ❧ ————

In the south of England, for intermittent fever, the patient is recommended to eat seven sage leaves on seven successive mornings, fasting meanwhile; and in northern Scotland scrofulous affections are thought to yield to the touch of a seventh son, when accompanied by an invocation of the Trinity.

———— ❧ ❧ ————

The belief in the magical curative qualities of the number nine was not limited to the northern nations. Thus the inhabitant of ancient Apulia, when bitten by a scorpion, proceeded to walk nine times around the walls of his native town.

The women of Canton, China, attribute magical properties for the cure of cutaneous affections to water drawn after midnight of the seventh day of the seventh month.

When a gypsy child bumps its head, a knife blade is first pressed upon the swelling, after which an incantation is pronounced three, seven, or nine times, and the knife is stuck into the earth a like number of times. Many charms employed by gypsies could be mentioned in illustration of the avoidance of even numbers in all their mystic rites.

# THE NUMBER THIRTEEN

In regard to the luck of odd numbers, the exception, which is commonly supposed to prove the rule, is the much maligned thirteen.

In the Scandinavian mythology Loki, the Principle of Evil and the chief author of human misfortunes, accompanied the twelve Aesir, or Demigods, and was reckoned the thirteenth among them. Moreover, the Valkyrs, or Virgins, who waited upon the heroes in Valhalla, were thirteen in number, and from these sources is believed to have sprung the very common superstition concerning the ill luck and fatality of the number thirteen, especially in connection with a party of guests at table.

---

The most generally received explanation of the origin of this popular belief refers it to the Last Supper of our Lord, where Judas is sometimes represented as the thirteenth guest. But why Judas rather than John, the beloved disciple? However, this is the generally accepted starting point of this notable superstition. As with the Jews the thirteenth month, and with the Christians the thirteenth day of the year, which began with Christmas, were accounted ominous, so, with the inhabitants of India, the thirteenth year was considered to be of evil import. It is evident, therefore, that the source of this nearly worldwide belief cannot be attributed wholly either to the mythology of the north or to the Paschal Supper.

---

When the year was reckoned as thirteen lunar months of twenty-eight days each, the number thirteen, according to one view, was considered auspicious; but when, under the present method of solar time, the number of months was reduced to twelve, thirteen's reputation was changed for the worse.

---

In early times the Feast of the Epiphany, which is the thirteenth day after Christmas Eve, was feared because at that time the three goddesses, Berchta, Holle, and Befana, with their ghostly companions, were especially active; and, as a guard against their machinations, the initial letters of the names of the three kings, or wise men, were written on many a door.

Of the former trio, Berchta was represented as a shaggy monster, whose name was used as a bugbear with which to frighten children. She was intrusted with the oversight of spinning, and on the eve of Epiphany she visited the homes of the countryfolk, distributing empty reels, which she required to be filled within a specified time; if her demands were not complied with, she retaliated by tangling and befouling the flax.

Holle, or Holda, was a benignant and merciful goddess, of an obliging disposition, who was usually most lenient, except when she noticed disorder in the affairs of a household. Her favorite resorts were the lakes and fountains, but she had also an oversight over domestic concerns, and shared with Berchta the supervision of spinning. Sometimes, however, she appeared as an old hag, with bristling, matted hair and long teeth.

Befana, the third goddess, was of Italian origin, and her name signifies Epiphany. On that day the women and children used to place a rag doll in the window in her honor. In personal appearance she was black and ugly, but her disposition was not unfriendly.

---

So universal has been the superstition regarding the number thirteen at table, that it has long been a matter of etiquette in France to avoid having exactly that number of guests at dinner parties. The Parisian *pique-assiette*, a person whose title corresponds to the English 'trencher friend' or 'sponger' is also known as a *quatorzième*, his chief mission being to occupy the fourteenth seat at a banquet.

---

The ancients, we learn, had ideas of their own regarding the proper size of festive gatherings, their favorite number of *convives* being between three and nine, the number of the Graces and Muses respectively.

---

Opinions have differed as to whether misfortune were likely to befall the whole company of thirteen persons rash enough to dine together, or only the one leaving the room first after the repast. All evil, however, was supposed to be averted by the entire company rising to their feet together. It has been wittily remarked that the only occasion when thirteen plates at table should cause disquietude is when the food is only sufficient for twelve persons.

---

At the thirteenth annual dinner of that unique organization, the Thirteen Club, held in New York city, January 13, 1895, at 7.13 p.m., the custodian delivered an address in which were recounted the circumstances of the club's formation. So prevalent was the apprehension of evil likely to result from the assembling together of thirteen persons that, when at length the requisite number were seated at table, it was found desirable to lock the doors of the banquet-room, lest some faint soul should retire abruptly.

Field-Marshal Lord Roberts, in his *Forty-One Years in India* mentions a circumstance occurring in his own experience, which affords evidence, were any needed, of the falsity of the superstition in question. On New Year's Day 1853, Lord Roberts was one of a party of thirteen who dined together at a staff officers' mess at Peshawar, on the Afghan frontier. Eleven years later all these officers were alive, the greater number having participated in the suppression of the great Sepoy Mutiny of 1857, during which several of them were wounded.

In Italy shrewd theatrical managers have found it expedient to change the number of Box 13 to 12a, and in many streets of Rome and Florence one may search in vain for house numbers between 12 ½ and 14. A gentleman of the writer's acquaintance, living in Washington D.C., sent a formal petition to the authorities asking leave to change the number of his house, for the sole reason that it contained the ominous figures.

As an illustration of the popular distrust of the number thirteen among the villagers of the Department of Ille-et-Villaine, France, may be cited the following custom, which is in vogue in that district. Children are there usually taught the art of knitting by devout elderly women. The little ones are first seated in a circle, and, to facilitate the work, on the completion of the first round of knitting they are made to

repeat the following words: '*One*, the Father'; at the close
of the second round, '*Two*, the Son;' and so on, as follows:
'*Three*, the Holy Spirit; the *four* Evangelists; the *five* wounds of
our Lord; the *six* commandments of the church; *seven* sacra-
ments; *eight* beatitudes; *nine* choirs of angels; *ten* commandments of God; *eleven* thousand virgins; *twelve* apostles;' and at
the close of the thirteenth round, the children mention the
name of Judas.

---

This remarkable and unreasonable prejudice against an
innocent number seems to pervade all classes and communities. The possession of intelligence and culture is no
effective barrier against it. Arguments and reasoning are
alike vain. Even at this writing, an evening journal records
that at a recent meeting of a newly elected board of aldermen
in an enlightened city of eastern Massachusetts, one of the
members objected to casting lots for seats because he did not
relish the idea of drawing number thirteen. However, his
scruples having been in a measure overcome, he was much
relieved to find that the number eleven, which is both uneven
and lucky, had fallen to his share.

---

Brand quotes as follows from Fuller's *Mixt Contemplations*
(1660) in reference to this subject:

> A covetous Courtier complained to King Edward
> the sixt of Christ Colledge in Cambridge, that
> it was a superstitious foundation, consisting of
> a Master and twelve Fellowes, in imitation of

Christ and His twelve Apostles. He advised the King also to take away one or two Fellowships, so as to discompose that superstitious number. 'Oh, no!' said the King, 'I have a better way than that to mar their conceit; I will add a thirteenth Fellowship unto them;' which he did accordingly, and so it remaineth unto this day.

———— ⚜ • ⚜ ————

Persians regard the number thirteen as so unlucky that they refrain from naming it. When they wish to allude to this number, instead of mentioning the proper term, they use words meaning 'much more' or 'nothing'.

———— ⚜ • ⚜ ————

In Scotland this number is known as the 'Deil's Dozen', a phrase which has been supposed to have some connection with card playing, there being thirteen cards in each suit of the 'Deil's Books'. John Jamieson, in his Scottish Dictionary, avows his inability to trace the superstition to its source, but believes that it includes the idea of the thirteenth being of the Devil's lot. The number thirteen is also sometimes known as a 'baker's dozen', because it was formerly a common practice to give thirteen loaves for twelve, the extra piece being called the *in-bread* or *to-bread*. This custom is supposed to have originated at a time when heavy fines were imposed for short weights, the additional bread being given by bakers as a precautionary measure.

———— ⚜ • ⚜ ————

In certain cases, contrary to the general rule, thirteen is accounted a fortunate numeral, or even as one possessing extraordinary virtues.

Dr Daniel G. Brinton, in *A Primer of Mayan Hieroglyphics* says that in the old language of the Mayas, an aboriginal tribe of Yucatan, the numbers nine and thirteen were used to denote indefinite greatness and supreme excellence. Thus a very fortunate man was possessed of nine souls, and the phrase, 'thirteen generations old', conveyed the idea of perpetuity. The 'Demon with thirteen powers' was a prominent figure in the mythology of the Tzentals, a Mayan tribe.

---

According to a widely prevalent popular impression, a brood is usually odd in number, and therefore it is folly to set an even number of eggs under a hen. In spite of the falsity of this idea, it is still quite customary to set thirteen eggs, an even number in this case being accounted unlucky.

---

Gerald Massey, in *The Natural Genesis*, remarks that 'there were thirteen kinds of spices set out in the Jewish religious service, along with the zodiacal number of twelve loaves of shew-bread. There are thirteen articles to the Hebrew faith, and the Cabalists have thirteen rules by which they are enabled to penetrate the mysteries of the Hebrew Scriptures. Thirteen are the dialectical canons of the Talmudical doctors for determining the sense of the law in all civil and ecclesiastical cases.

---

In England the day of twenty-four hours was formerly divided into thirteen parts, as follows:

1. After midnight.
2. Cock-crow.
3. Between the first cock-crow and daybreak.
4. The dawn.
5. Morning.
6. Noon.
7. Afternoon.
8. Sunset.
9. Twilight.
10. Evening.
11. Candletime.
12. Bedtime.
13. Dead of night.

Recurring now to the prevalent notions regarding the sinister and portentous character of this number, one may well inquire in all seriousness whether the harboring of this and other firmly rooted superstitious fancies is compatible with a deep and abiding Christian faith. The answer is plainly in the negative. Therefore it is doubtless true – and the truth should make us free – that the greater our indifference to the various alleged omens and auguries which so easily beset us, the more readily shall we acquire and retain a firm and enduring dependence on Divine Providence.

# HESPERUS PRESS

—◄○►—

Under our three imprints, Hesperus Press publishes over 300 books by many of the greatest figures in worldwide literary history, as well as contemporary and debut authors well worth discovering.

## HESPERUS CLASSICS

handpicks the best of worldwide and translated literature, introducing forgotten and neglected books to new generations.

## HESPERUS NOVA

showcases quality contemporary fiction and non-fiction designed to entertain and inspire.

## HESPERUS MINOR

rediscovers well-loved children's books from the past – these are books which will bring back fond memories for adults, which they will want to share with their children and loved ones.

To find out more visit www.hesperuspress.com
@HesperusPress

# THE
# LADIES'
## BOOK OF
# ETIQUETTE
## AND MANUAL OF
# POLITENESS

## £7.99 · FLORENCE HARTLEY

*What do you do if you notice a stranger's dress is tucked up at the back?*

*How should you react if you find a worm in your food at a dinner party?*

*And what on earth do you wear when you're invited to a ball?*

If these questions baffle you, fear not, my good lady! This guide contains the answers to all these tricky questions and many more.

With this trusty book in hand, you need never worry about awkward situations again. Becoming a true and polite lady is simple — just sit back, relax and delve into this treasure trove of tips. But no slouching!

# THE
# GENTLEMEN'S
## BOOK OF
# ETIQUETTE
## AND MANUAL OF
# POLITENESS

**£7.99 · CECIL B. HARTLEY**

*What do you do in polite society if you find an insect in your food?*

*How should a gentleman ask a lady to dance?*

*And what on earth is the etiquette for smoking cigars?*

Ever found yourself baffled by such delicate questions of etiquette? Do not fret, for this gentlemen's guide will provide the answer to these conundrums and many more.

So when you retire to the drawing room with your port after supper, be sure to settle down with this indispensable volume full of advice for the discerning gentleman.

| Author | Title | Foreword |
|--------|-------|----------|

## AUTOBIOGRAPHY & BIOGRAPHY

| Author | Title | Foreword |
|--------|-------|----------|
| Albinati, Edoardo | Coming Back | |
| Aubrey, John | Lives of Eminent Men | Ruth Scurr |
| Aubrey, John | Scientific Lives | Ruth Scurr |
| Borden, Mary | Forbidden Zone, The | Malcolm Brown |
| Brooke, Rupert | Letters from America | Benjamin Markovits |
| Garibaldi, Giuseppe | My Life | Tim Parks |
| Kennedy, Richard | Boy at the Hogarth Press, A | John Randle |
| Machiavelli, Nicolò | Life of Castruccio Castracani | Richard Overy |
| Northup, Solomon | 12 Years a Slave | |
| Stendhal | Letters to Pauline | Adam Thirlwell |
| Tagore, Rabindranath | Boyhood Days | Amartya Sen |
| Voltaire | Memoirs of the life of Monsieur de Voltaire | Ruth Scurr |
| Woolf, Virginia | Platform of Time, The | |
| Zweig, Stefan | Nietzsche | |

## FOOD & DRINK

| Author | Title | Foreword |
|--------|-------|----------|
| Bradley, Alice | Candy Cookbook, The | |
| Thomas, Jerry | How to Mix Drinks or The Bon Vivant's Companion | |

## HISTORY & REFERENCE

| Author | Title | Foreword |
|--------|-------|----------|
| Aldrich, Mildred | Hilltop on the Marne, A | |
| Evans, Edward Payson | Animal Trials | |

| | | |
|---|---|---|
| Grose, Francis | Dictionary of the Vulgar Tongue, The | |
| Hartley, Cecil B. | Gentlemen's Book of Etiquette, and Manual of Politeness, The | |
| Hartley, Florence | Ladies Book of Etiquette, and Manual of Politeness, The | |
| Mayhew, Henry | Wayward Genius of Henry Mayhew, The: Pioneering Reportage from Victorian London | |
| Wharton, Edith | Fighting France: from Dunkerque to Belfort | Colm Tóibín |

## LITERARY/CULTURAL STUDIES & ESSAYS

| | | |
|---|---|---|
| da Vinci, Leonardo | Prophecies | Eraldo Affinati |
| Lamb, Charles | Essays of Elia | Matthew Sweet |
| Margolyes, Miriam; Fraser, Sonia | Dickens' Women | |
| Poe, Edgar Allan | Eureka | Sir Patrick Moore |
| Rilke, Rainer Maria & Betz, Maurice | Rilke in Paris | |
| Stendhal | Memoirs of an Egotist | Doris Lessing |
| Swift, Jonathan | Directions to Servants | Colm Tóibín |
| Swift, Jonathan | Polite Conversation | Toby Litt |
| Tyler, Daniel | Guide to Dickens' London, A | |
| Woolf, Virginia | Hyde Park Gate News | Hermione Lee |
| Woolf, Virginia | Carlyle's House and Other Sketches | Doris Lessing |
| Wren, Jenny | Lazy Thoughts of a Lazy Girl | Jenny Éclair |

# POLITICS

| | |
|---|---|
| Swisher, Clayton E. | Palestine Papers: The End of The Road? The |
| Kushner, Barry | Who Needs the Cuts? |
| & Saville | |

# TRAVEL WRITING

| | | |
|---|---|---|
| Byron, Robert | Europe in the Looking Glass | Jan Morris |
| Collins, Wilkie; | Lazy Tour of Two Idle Apprentices, The | |
| Dickens, Charles | | |
| Fitzgerald, F. Scott | Cruise of the Rolling Junk, The | Paul Theroux |
| Levi, Carlo | Essays on India | Anita Desai |
| Levi, Carlo | Words are Stones | Anita Desai |
| Mayakovsky, Vladimir | My Discovery of America | Colum McCann |
| Miller, Henry | Aller Retour New York | |
| Zweig, Stefan | Journeys | |